ANGLICAN HERITAGE:
THEOLOGY AND SPIRITUALITY

Bishop Lyttelton
Library
Winchester

Among other books by the same author:

THE EUCHARISTIC THEOLOGY OF JEREMY TAYLOR TODAY (1988)

ANGLICAN HERITAGE:
Theology and Spirituality

H. R. McADOO
Formerly Archbishop of Dublin

The Canterbury Press
Norwich

Copyright © H. R. McAdoo, 1991

First published 1991 by
The Canterbury Press Norwich
(a publishing imprint of Hymns Ancient & Modern Limited,
a Registered Charity)
St Mary's Works, St Mary's Plain,
Norwich, Norfolk, NR3 3BH

**A catalogue record for this book is available
from the British Library**

ISBN 1-85311-045-0

Typeset by Cambridge Composing UK Limited
and printed in Great Britain by
St Edmundsbury Press, Suffolk

Contents

Contents

Introductory Note

The purpose of this book is to enable us to hear a voice from our own past. We need to learn that the process of remembering, of ongoing corporate recollection, is an element essential to our self-understanding. Two years ago a distinguished theologian wrote to me that by neglecting or ignoring our Anglican heritage 'our Church seems to be behaving like some poor person suffering total loss of memory'.

That heritage has in large measure made us what we are and is a factor enabling us to become what we truly are in Christ through the Spirit. The book is therefore meant to be an exercise in self-understanding.

In that exercise our community memory plays a significant role. To listen to a voice from our own past is not to engage in historical quarrying for its own sake. Nor is it to indulge in a sort of historical nostalgia. Rather is it to make clear to ourselves why it is that we go about what St Bernard called 'the business of all businesses' in a particular way.

It is to call to mind, in company with Christians of all traditions, our failure to present at their best those good things we have inherited. It is to remember that even the best parts of our inheritance are but imperfect instruments for the proclamation of the Gospel of Jesus Christ, the living Lord.

That the voice from our past evokes clear echoes for Anglicanism today and in the inter-Church scene is the theme of the 'Postscript from the Present'.

H. R. McADOO

I

The Anglican Ethos

'There is no Church whose every part so squares unto my conscience . . . as the Church of England'
— Sir Thomas Browne

WHAT I am endeavouring to do in this book is to conduct some sort of investigation into the nature and the sources of our Anglican heritage. It is an attempt at the detection of what it is that makes Anglicanism what it is, spiritually and theologically. *I suppose you might describe it an an exercise in self-understanding.* Basically, what informs and controls the Church at all levels of its proclamation and practice is 'the faith once for all delivered' (Jude, 3), the good news of the living Lord, Jesus Christ who is 'the same yesterday, today and for ever' (Heb.13.8). But the Church is obviously in time and space, embedded in history, its past affecting its present and its vision for the future. So its experience of and interpretation of the unchanging Gospel is necessarily expressed in terms comprehensible to each generation in its geographical location and stage of cultural development. Thus, the faith as received, understood and proclaimed by Anglicanism is propounded in what one might call an idiom which reflects its historical and cultural background as well as its present situation. This, of course, is true in varying degrees of every Christian Church – inevitably so, since the faith once for all delivered is not delivered to or by disembodied spirits but to and by men and women who are part and parcel of that amalgam of time and movements which we call history. The more I consider this project the more convinced I am that it cannot aspire to be a picture. *It can only be an impressionist sketch*, suggesting in broad strokes and in necessarily selective detail something of the whole, but quite unable to encompass it in its depth and richness.

It seems to me that the most profitable approach to this exercise in self-understanding *will be along two merging paths, an investigation of theology and an investigation of practice.* What in fact then we are doing is taking a survey of the seventeenth-century scene with a view to answering the fundamental questions 'What sort of thinking and what sort of religion are involved in this heritage of ours?' *What did it look like and what made it look that way,* and *how much of this heritage remains part of the way in which Anglicans today do theology, offer worship and relate to other Christians?*

The thinking comes first, for a religion is dyed the colour of its deepest thoughts. Paradoxically, at first sight, the basis of Anglican self-understanding is the assertion that *there is no such thing as the Anglican faith.* There is only 'the faith once for all delivered', taught, proclaimed and (through grace) lived, by Anglicans. There is only the Catholic faith, as set out in the New Testament and summarised in the Creeds. This is of the essence of Anglicanism which, unlike Roman Catholicism or some forms of Calvinism, refuses to affirm as *de fide* and necessarily part of its identity any doctrine not so qualified in or by Scripture or by the Primitive Church. This deliberate travelling light is the expression of the Anglican desire to preserve and propagate the whole Gospel and nothing but the Gospel. It lies behind the refusal to make essential, for example, the Marian dogmas or extreme teachings on election and reprobation.

This is a constant in Anglican thinking, taking different shapes but remaining unchanged in content. From the *Reports* of the Lambeth Conferences of 1948 and 1968, it reaches back to the sixteenth century. Matthew Parker, Archbishop of Canterbury from 1559 to 1575 'saw his Church securely anchored doctrinally in Scripture and the Fathers and he allowed no severance, but rather asserted unbroken continuity between the Early Church and the Church of England. Parker wrote in 1564 to Sir William Cecil about a conversation with the French Ambassador and the Bishop of Coutances that "in fine they professed that we were in religion very nigh to them. I answered that I would wish them to come nigher to us, *grounding ourselves (as we do) upon the Apostolic doctrine and pure time of the Primitive Church".*[1] We meet exactly the same statement of position in John Jewel's *Apologia* which I have described elsewhere as 'one of the earliest, if not the earliest, essay in Anglican self-understanding'. He wrote 'We have returned to the Apostles and old Catholic fathers. *We have planted no new religion, but only have preserved the old* that was undoubtedly founded and used by the Apostles of Christ and other holy Fathers of the Primitive Church'. He insisted that 'this lawful Reformation . . . is *so* far from taking from us the name or nature of true Catholics . . . or depriving us of the fellowship of the apostolic Church or impairing the right faith, sacraments, priesthood and governance of the Catholic Church that it hath cleared and settled them on us'.[2]

This central affirmation is not only the constantly-expressed view of Anglican theologians but has been incorporated into our official formularies. The Preamble and Declaration in the Constitution of the Church of Ireland, drawn up in 1870, affirming that the Church is Catholic and Apostolic, asserts that the Church of Ireland 'doth continue to profess the faith of Christ as professed by the Primitive Church'. It affirms that the Church is Reformed because it deliberately rejects all doctrinal innovations 'whereby the Primitive Faith hath been from time to time defaced or overlaid'. Similarly, the Irish Preface of 1878 to the Book of Common Prayer notes that 'it contained the true doctrine of Christ, and a pure manner and order of Divine Service, according to the Holy Scriptures and the practice of the Primitive Church'. One recalls the aphorism of John Cosin, driven into exile by Cromwell: 'Protestant and Reformed according to the Ancient Catholic Church'.

I have dwelt on this because it is a formative element in our Anglican heritage. Lancelot Andrewes (1555–1626) summed it up concisely: 'One canon . . . two testaments, three creeds, four general councils, five centuries and the series of the Fathers in that period . . . determine the boundary of our faith'.[3] It is a position which has the great merit of *simplicity without shallowness*. An American writer has called it 'a preference for an economy of essential doctrine'.[4] The distinctiveness of Anglican thinking lies not in beliefs or doctrines regarded as being characteristic of Anglicanism. Rather does the distinctiveness lie in an insistence on 'the faith once for all delivered' of which Scripture and the faith of the Primitive Church form the criteria.[5] This is why, early in the 17th century, Archbishop Laud affirmed that Catholicity was not in a 'narrow conclave' and so the purpose of his book is 'to lay open those wider gates of the Catholic Church, confined to no age, time or place; *nor knowing any bounds but that faith which was once (and but once for all) delivered to the Saints*'.[6] This is why, at the end of the century, Archbishop Wake, who corresponded with Reformed and Roman Catholic theologians, made it clear that this was the distinctively Anglican basis: 'our Church stands upon a different bottom from most of those in which the system-writers have been bred'.[7]

I do not know a better description of what the Anglican heritage in thinking and religious practice (*our two merging approaches*) than that of Jeremy Taylor (1613–1667), dispossessed priest of a persecuted Church, who was to become one of the glories of the Anglican tradition. Driven from his parish, in poverty, forbidden with all his fellows, to use the Prayer Book and to celebrate the sacraments, he wrote:

'What can be supposed wanting (in our Church) in order to salvation? We have the Word of God, the Faith of the Apostles, the Creeds of the Primitive Church, the Articles of the four first General Councils, a holy liturgy, excellent prayers, perfect sacraments, faith and repentance, the Ten Commandments, and the sermons of Christ, and all the precepts and counsels of the Gospels. We teach the necessity of good works, and require and strictly exact the severity of a holy life. We live in obedience to God, and are ready to die for Him, and do so when He requires us so to do . . . We worship Him at the mention of His holy name. We confess His attributes. We love His servants. We pray for all men. We love all Christians, even our most erring brethren. We confess our sins to God and to our brethren whom we have offended, and to God's ministers in cases of scandal or of a troubled conscience. We communicate often . . . our priests absolve the penitent. Our Bishops ordain priests and confirm baptised persons, and bless their people and intercede for them. And what could here be wanting to salvation?[8]

Taylor wrote that when things were at a low ebb yet his confidence in the Anglican heritage and his charity towards other Christians never wavered. Triumphalism or complacency in any form is to be deplored and while we love our Church, warts and all, we also love our brethren of the Roman and the Reformed traditions. We have much to learn from both and from the riches they have severally brought to the Christian inheritance.

The Hapax and Development

As we analyse the ethos of Anglicanism, which continues theologically much the same now as in the period we are investigating, one question may strike the contemporary mind. Does this continuing emphasis on the *hapax*, the once-for-allness of the faith, exclude any development, leaving us with a fossilized religion? This is something that must be looked at in the interests of our self-understanding. It is a necessary clarification. The *Report* of Lambeth 1968 in its section on renewal in faith places the question firmly in the context of the guidance of the Spirit abiding in the Church: 'This faith, which is set forth uniquely in the Scriptures and is summed up in the Catholic Creeds, *develops and grows under the guidance of the Holy Spirit* within the life of the Church, the Body of Christ'.[9] The preamble to the section speaks of the church's need for 'a renewed awareness of the Gospel . . . a deeper awareness of the deposit of the faith once delivered to the Saints'.[10]

What does this mean? If revelation is, so to speak, closed since 'in this final age he has spoken to us in the Son' (Heb.1.2), what meaning can development have for Anglicans? I think that the solution lies, first, in realising that God continues to

5

speak to us in Jesus, the living Lord, through the Spirit. This requires of his people in every age that the living revelation must be proclaimed, re-presented, apprehended and appropriated in all the changes and varieties of human cultures throughout the course of history.

This is a very different idea of development because it is development *from* the facts and content of the revelation, not development *away* from them. One may take as examples the fourth-century development of the Catholic doctrine of the Trinity, or theories of the atonement, whether in the middle ages, the reformation period or later still. In both instances, the facts are part of the Christian revelation in a way that, for example, the dogma of the Assumption is not. The criteria are to be found in Holy Scripture and in the living tradition comformable to Scripture. Otherwise, speculation takes over and you have what R. P. C. Hanson called 'a virtually uncontrolled doctrinal space flight'. In other words, the Christian revelation has a dynamic of life demanding constant re-presentation and deepening awareness but always under the check of Holy Scripture. Elsewhere in the same lectures, Hanson likens this development to a boat moored to a fixed buoy; 'There is a point at which the cable attached to the buoy always checks its course, not always pulling it back to the same point, but always preventing it moving any further on its existing course'.[11]

This is saying that 'the faith once for all delivered' is not something propositional. Rather is it something living and entire and growing, not in the sense of having things added on to it, but growing and deepening in the way in which successive generations apprehend and proclaim 'the unsearchable riches of Christ' (Eph.3.8). The Anglican position was well expressed by Michael Ramsey: 'Developments then took place, but they were all tested. The tests of a true development are whether it bears witness to the gospel, whether it expresses the general consciousness of the Christians, and whether it serves the organic unity of the Body in all its parts. These tests are summed up in the Scriptures, wherein the historical gospel and the experience of the redeemed and the nature of the one Body are described. Hence, while the Canon of Scripture is in itself a development, it has a special authority to control and to check the whole field of development in life and doctrine'.[12]

I hope then as we try to carry out this exercise in self-understanding that we are seeing from a different angle why the Anglican formularies give the primary place to Scripture, insisting that whatever is not contained in it or consonant with it cannot be required of any man as necessary to salvation (Article IV). Thus, while the Church is described as 'a witness and keeper of holy Writ' it cannot enforce as *de fide* any doctrinal development which is not conformable to it (Article XX).

This leads us straight to tradition and the role it plays in Anglican understanding of the Faith and in the Community of faith.

The Place of Tradition in Anglican Thinking

There are the frequent references both by theologians and in official formularies to the faith and practice of 'the Primitive Church'. How primitive is 'primitive' and what is the function of appealing to tradition? What do Anglicans understand by 'tradition'? I think that we make the matter clear by recalling that the Church is the 'witness and keeper' of Scripture, standing in the same relationship to it as that of a judge to the law. He administers and interprets the law but is himself subject to the law and can neither add to it nor take from it. This process by which the living Church interprets and enters into the meaning of the faith once for all delivered is tradition. This continuous exposition and experience is controlled by Scripture. It was Henry Parry Liddon, the great second-generation Tractarian, who wrote 'We cannot separate the Bible from the Church which recognized and has preserved it. The Divine Book and the Divine Society are the two factors of the one Revelation – *each checking the other*'.[13] Tradition then for Anglicans means

7

tradition which is conformable to Scripture. This is made abundantly clear by Articles XX and XXXIV and this is why Scripture and the teaching and practice of the Primitive Church are explicitly linked in the Constitution of the Church of Ireland.[14] *The reason is, of course, that the Primitive Church proved the rule of faith from the Scriptures.* Francis White (1564?–1638), Bishop of Ely, put it in a nutshell: 'We reject not all Traditions, but such as are . . . not consonant to the prime rule of faith, to wit, the Holy Scripture. Genuine traditions agreeable to the Rule of Faith, subservient to piety, consonant with Holy Scripture, derived from the Apostolical times by a successive current, and which have the uniform testimony of pious Antiquity, are received and honoured by us'.[15] More than any, however, it was Lancelot Andrewes who presented the appeal to antiquity in a positive form as an essential element in Anglican apologetic.

Now we can see why the Anglican emphasis on 'primitive' is of great practical importance as a guarantee that the Church is at all times proclaiming the original, the authentic faith and nothing else. The martyred Laud put it this way: 'I believe both Scripture and Creed in the same uncorrupted sense which the primitive Church believed them; and am sure that I do so believe them, because I cross not in my belief anything delivered by the primitive Church'.[16]

The function of the Anglican appeal to antiquity is both faith-guarding and identity-affirming. Taking consonancy with the original deposit of faith as the standard it affirms identity with the Primitive Church in terms of a living continuity of faith and order: 'Let that be accounted the true Church, whose Faith and Doctrine is most conformable and agreeable with the Primitive'.[17]

As we continue this evaluation of our heritage it is becoming apparent that 'simplicity without shallowness' is an honest characterisation of the Anglican ethos. William Chillingworth (1602–1644) claimed that the truths of salvation are of an 'admirable simplicity'. I would see two other constituents in the Anglican affirmation of the faith which appear to me to be confirmatory of this assessment.

Fundamentals

The first is what *The Malta Report* (6) of the Joint Preparatory Anglican/Roman Catholic Commission called 'the Anglican distinction of fundamentals from non-fundamentals'. It is a distinction which runs through the theology of the period from Hooker onwards and is the preserve of no group but common to all the Anglican writers. The concept must derive from the conviction, expressed for example in the Articles, that only what is necessary for salvation can be *de fide*, mandatory for Christian believing and behaving. With one voice seventeenth-century Anglican theologians claimed the Creeds to be the summing up of what is necessary. Other matters, accessories, were less determinate and varied in importance and in authority for the believer. This theme of the distinction between fundamentals and non-fundamentals and its link with the *hapax*, the once-for-allness of the faith, is everywhere in seventeenth-century Anglicanism. For Jeremy Taylor in his *Liberty of Prophesying* (1647) it is the only live option by which to achieve 'unity of faith'.[18]

The distinction is far from being *simplistic* and bears a certain interesting resemblance to the concept of a hierarchy of truths which is to be found in the *Decree on Ecumenism (II)* of Vatican II. Further, the content of the term fundamental and the ranking, so to speak, of accessory truths both need to be appreciated. Early in the century Archbishop Laud dealt with this and later on at the turn of the century his successor Archbishop Wake made some sophisticated comments on the matter. In fact, Wake wrote to one of his French correspondents that it was Laud 'who beyond any other undertook the defence' of the view shared by them both.

The question is just as relevant to today's inter-Church scene as it was to that of yesterday, so I hope I may be forgiven for quoting something I wrote about it elsewhere. Archbishop Wake (1657–1737), a skilled negotiator and administrator was also an able theologian and had been in his youth a chaplain in Paris: 'In his letters on Christian unity to Reformed theologians and to the Gallicans alike, he set out the same principle in either case. It is, in his view, an indispensable prerequisite to any effective discussion of unity. The questions which we have been considering namely, *What are the fundamentals*, and, *Where is doctrine to be found*, exercised Wake as they do theologians today. Wake's perceptiveness here is keen and it is strikingly matched by Laud. In a letter of 1719 to the reformed theologian Turrettini, Wake wrote that he had 'come at last to this opinion; that the peace of Christendom can no way be restored but by separating the fundamental articles of our religion (in which almost all churches agree) from others, which in their several natures *though not strictly fundamental*, may yet be of more, or less, moment to us in the way of our salvation'. Wake sees a gradation from fundamentals through matters 'not strictly fundamental' but not to be lightly dismissed from 'the truths of faith'. This has about it more than a suggestion of the hierarchy of truths which would be set out two and a half centuries later in the Second Vatican Council's decree on ecumenism (II): 'When comparing doctrines, they should remember that in Catholic teaching there exists an order or 'hierarchy' of truths, since they vary in their relationship to the foundation of the Christian faith'.

More remarkable still is the similarity here of Laud's wording on the same point: 'And yet for all this, everything fundamental is *not of a like nearness to the foundation, nor of equal primeness in the faith.* And my granting the Creed to be fundamental doth not deny but that there are *quaedam prima credibilia*, certain prime principles of faith, in the bosom whereof all other articles lay wrapped and folded up'.

Wake makes the same point requiring a closer look at the content of the term 'fundamental'. He writes 'It is indeed a work of greater difficulty, not to say danger, to distinguish the essential articles of doctrine from the rest, in such wise that nothing in them is either superfluous or lacking; that nothing essential to salvation is omitted, nor anything non-essential included in the number of essentials'. This is acute and very up-to-date and relevant analysis. What were Wake and Laud getting at? My view is that both were affirming that funda-

mentals, still scripturally revealed, include certain scriptur-
ally-warranted essentials in the life of the Church, namely the
sacraments and a ministry to administer them. One has only
to read Laud's *Conference* and Wake's correspondence and the
great mass of seventeenth-century writing on these subjects,
to see that for these men, without baptism, without the Bread
and the Book, without a ministry, there could be no Church
. . . the whole weight of Anglican theology and appeal to
antiquity surely confirms that fundamentals must include
that without which the household of faith could have no
existence'.[19]

With our second constituent, the appeal to reason, the end
of this attempt to sketch the outlines of the Anglican heritage
begins to come into view as far as the investigation of the
thinking, the theological method, is concerned.

The Appeal to Reason

Most Christians think that while faith and reason may have at
times an uneasy relationship yet they can claim that Christianity is basically a reasonable faith. With Lancelot Andrewes,
however, they would agree that while 'we must try and prove
those things which we thus receive'. . . yet 'when we have thus
strengthened our faith we must yet look for a higher teacher'.[20]
The appeal to reason, which is part of the threefold Anglican
appeal to Scripture, tradition and reason, by its nature *implies
choice and freedom*. The appeal to reason is everywhere in the
Anglican heritage from Richard Hooker (1554?–1600) to Lambeth 1968 which insists that 'the inheritance of faith' implies an
authority which 'refuses to insulate itself against . . . the free
action of reason' and which, to be credible, requires 'credentials
in a shape which corresponds to the requirements of reason'.[21]
Sometimes one gets the impression that people regard the
appeal to reason as a modern phenomenon and that it was the
Lux Mundi group which invented a liberal Catholicism in 1889!

The fact is that from Hooker onwards the stress on reason
and on a certain liberality is endemic in Anglicanism. Hooker's book, the *Ecclesiastical Polity* (1592,1594?) can in one sense

be described as a defence of reason. As against the Puritan position typified by the *Admonition to the parliament* (1572), he was advocating a liberal method which holds reason to be competent to deal with matters of ecclesiastical polity and to be in itself an ultimate factor in theology. This is the core of the first Book of the *Polity* and the third Book has a long section showing the danger to religion of disparaging reason. It is a seminal book and many books have since been written about it. There passed from it into the developing theological method of the seventeenth century something indelible. Hooker's delineation of a liberal method in theology keeping company with what he called 'the absolute perfection of Scripture'[22] and 'the judgment of antiquity'[23] became and remained the model. His work was widely influential, not only on theologians, but on laypeople like the saintly Accountant-General of Ireland, James Bonnell, and his not so saintly fellow civil servant Samuel Pepys. Pepys borrowed the *Polity* from a friend, who, he tells us, 'chawed tobacco' for his health and liked the book so much that he bought his own copy. With Hooker, the three-fold appeal became fully established. Aware of the limitations of reason, he could still write 'such as the evidence is . . . such is the heart's assent thereunto'.[24] James Bonnell described him as one who wrote 'with a primitive spirit but *modern judgment* and correctness'.[25] In fact, he has put his finger on the point: Hooker was trying to bring religion and theology into the modern world of his time by attempting to set reason and faith in an integrated view of life which implied some sort of unified idea of experience. Thomas Aquinas had sought a similar synthesis in his own day and setting, refusing 'to do violence to the autonomy of reason in its own sphere'.[26]

It is fascinating to see how, for instance, Archbishop Laud draws together the different threads, reason, fundamentals and the three-fold appeal into one pattern of believing: 'All points of doctrine, generally received as fundamental are established by Scripture, Creeds, and the first four General Councils, and thus there is need for no other certainty and reason so asserts'.[27] He insists that 'grace is never placed but in a reasonable creature'[28] and while faith is essential to Christian religion 'this light, when it hath made reason submit itself, clears the eye of reason: *it never puts it out*'.[29] Suprisingly to those who derive their picture of William Laud from potted histories, he shows a generous understanding of the intellectual problems of individual believers, speaking of 'a latitude in faith, especially in reference to different men's salvation: but to set a bound to this . . . just thus far you must believe in every particular, or incur damnation, is no work for my pen'. He refuses in his own words to take upon himself to 'shut any Christian out of heaven' because God's gifts 'to particular men are so various'. The only exception is 'the denial of the foundation' which puts one outside the community of faith.[30] In other words, there are boundary-markers. The Doctrine Commission's *Report* (1981) put it this way (p.44): 'As an individual I am of course free to believe what I like . . . but in so far as I am a member of the Church, I associate myself with a "corporate believing" which consists in a recognition of, and a constantly changing response to, "the authority of Scripture".' This is a very different picture of Laud from that created by his enemy Prynne or the legend created later by Lord Macaulay whose 'influence is in inverse ratio to his historical accuracy'.[31]

This theme of reason in theology, so firmly established by Hooker, gathered its own momentum as the century progressed and with variations in emphasis has remained part of the Anglican heritage. One may recall the Oxford school of rational theologians gathered around Lucius Cary, Lord Falkland, at his house in Great Tew near Oxford. This group, assembled before the Civil War, made the house resemble the University, to quote Hyde who was a member with people like Sheldon, Morley, Hammond, Hales, Chillingworth and others. Thus there were included in it men of the theological right and the theological left but together they reacted against a theology of authorities in favour of a theology which in John Hales's words was engaged in 'soundly discovering and laying down the truth of things'.[32] In a sentence, they strove to free their thinking by means of rational enquiry from the systematized statements of the Reformation and the Counter-Reformation. With Falkland and Chillingworth they adhered to what was plain and therefore necessary in Scripture and with Hales they felt that 'the sense is Scripture rather than the words' and to deal with it 'as chemists deal with natural bodies, torturing them to extract out of them that which God and nature never put in them' is meaningless for real religion. Scripture interprets the interpreter.[33] The fundamentals are clear, he says, and as to non-essentials he commends a modest scepticism 'till the remainder of our knowledge be supplied by Christ'.[34] The Civil War scattered them, claiming Falkland's life at the battle of Newbury in 1643 and driving others into retreat or exile but their work made a statement which was not lost sight of despite the troubled story which followed of a dispossessed and persecuted Church.

During the Protectorate another group of younger men, the Cambridge Platonists, were at work in a society where, slowly, the new naturalists and scientists were beginning to seek an alternative to Aristotelianism while the more profound religious thinkers were reacting against the current Augustinianism and a theology of word-spinning in which reason was regarded as suspect. More, Cudworth, Whichcote and Smith, despite a certain mystical aloofness, were probably more subtly influential on the tone of Anglican religious thought and practice than were their successors the Latitudinarians or the earlier Tew Circle. This, I would suggest, was because their concept of reason seems to include the notion of experience and because, however dimly, they were the first to visualise a changing world in which theology would have to come to terms with philosophy and science and a developing understanding of human experience. It was More, the most mystical of them all, who wrote 'To take away reason is to rob Christianity of that special prerogative it has above all other religions in the world, namely, that it dares appeal unto reason'.[35]

Books have been written about this very remarkable group and I content myself with the comment that 'their criticism (of current theological systems) was a new criticism in depth, and their picture of reason seemed to be three-dimensional too, having about it both warmth and colour. It seemed to be at home in the visible world as compared with the rather cold intellectualism of Tew which appeared to belong more in the study'.[36]

When we turn to Jeremy Taylor (1613–1667) we are looking at possibly the most intelligent and certainly one of the most learned of Anglican theologians whom literary critics have not hesitated to claim as one of the geniuses of English literature. His devotional writings have continued to be read down to our own times and you can still buy modern editions of his *Holy Living*. His moral theology anticipated most of the twentieth-century developments and his eucharistic theology strikes chords for the modern reader. Perhaps it is his independence of mind and the feeling he conveys of being at times our contemporary that is most striking. What bears most on our present theme is Taylor's refusal to accept the Augustinianism of his day on the subject of original sin and his determination to bring faith and reason into a relationship in which a reasonable mind can think theologically: 'If I find that all things satisfy my reason, I believe him saying that God said so, and then *pistis* or faith enters'.[37] Both the meaning of original sin, and the relationship between faith and reason, and the extent of free-dom, are discussed at length by Taylor in three major works, *Ductor Dubitantium*, *Unum Necessarium* and *Deus Justificatus*. For the purpose of our theme here it is enough to give one quotation from yet another of his works, *The Liberty of Prophesying*, which plainly shows the importance for him of reason in the threefold appeal which is always and explicitly Taylor's theological method: 'Scripture, tradition, councils, and fathers, are the evidence in a question, but reason is the judge'.[38] For him reason was not just ratiocination but 'a transcendent that runs through all topics'. It involves experience and he likens it to 'a box of quicksilver'. 'Our reason' he says 'does not consist in a mathematical point: and the heart of reason, that vital and most sensible part ... is an ambulatory essence, and not fixed'.[39] Taylor was a High Churchman, Laud's chaplain, but a friend of Chillingworth and More, and influenced by

Grotius. If one tries to fit him into a slot, he defies classification. In today's terms, 'liberal Catholic' might be an approximate description but we are still left with what his friend Rust called 'the largeness and freedom of his spirit'. That too has passed into the Anglican heritage, to its enrichment.

The Latitudinarians have tended to receive a bad press ('he is a gentleman of a wide swallow'),[40] but this on the whole is unfair. They were part of a changing social order in which science and the natural sciences were rapidly engaging men's minds. The Royal Society had been established and the range of data about the physical universe was steadily increasing. This had its effect not only on the way in which theological questions were considered but on the style and very language in which they were asked, as Bishop Sprat, historian of the Society, observed. The Latitudinarians recognized that a different kind of world was emerging and they sought to commend a religion relevant to the realities of men's lives and which would commend itself to men's free acceptance by its reasonableness. With them, the mystic experiential reason of the Cambridge Platonists has been tansmuted into reasonableness, at times almost appearing to be the appeal to common sense. They served their day and generation and although they may have made an entrance for Deism they made it possible for reasonable contemporaries to think theologically. They remained firmly Anglican in their use of the appeal to Scripture, tradition and reason. The standard of assay, says the greatest of them, Stillingfleet, is 'Scripture, reason or the consent of the Primitive Church'[41] But there is a shift of emphasis: the subtitle of his book *A Rational Account* shows that it is a vindication of Laud's *Conference*, an impressive demonstration of the unity and cohesion of seventeenth-century Anglicanism considering their respective view-points. The shift of emphasis is indicated by the title *A Rational Account* and by Stillingfleet's explicit choice of the clear style made popular by the Royal Society. While he supports Laud's thesis that Anglicans agree with the Fathers, holding the same concept of the relation of Scripture to fundamentals and doing theology by rational inference from the evidence as

Hooker had laid down, Stillingfleet takes the basic theme in the *Conference*, that of authority, and strives to establish a viable relationship between authority and reason. This he does because in an unsettling age of new discoveries no solution is acceptable which discounts the role of reason and 'the rational inducements which do incline the mind to a firm assent'. His discussion of 'saving faith' and intellectual persuasion brings the whole debate about as far as any moderns have brought it.[42]

The Anglican ethos is then one in which the given faith and the freedom of one's mind within those parameters have drawn to it many distinguished people around the world and countless others like that correspondent in a recent *Church Times* issue who, with her husband and three teenagers became Anglicans because 'one of the glories of the Anglican Church is that one *is* permitted to think things out for oneself, and therefore the God that one finds at the end of this is a personal God'.[43]

We recall Archbishop William Temple's excellent definition of the Anglican identity: 'Our special character and, as we believe, our peculiar contribution to the Universal Church, arises from the fact that, owing to historic circumstances, we have been enabled to combine in our one fellowship the traditional Faith and Order of the Catholic Church with that immediacy of approach to God through Christ to which the Evangelical Churches especially bear witness, and *freedom of intellectual inquiry*, whereby the correlation of the Christian revelation and advancing knowledge is constantly effected'.[44]

Taking into account and allowing for the totally different world of the twentieth century with all that has happened to human thinking and understanding, to religion and to theology, I would in the changed circumstances of our times give much the same sort of reasons for being an Anglican as did Sir Thomas Browne in 1642–3: 'There is no Church whose every part so squares unto my conscience, whose articles, constitutions, and customes seem so consonant unto reason, and as it were framed to my particular devotion, as this whereof I hold my beliefe, the Church of England ... In briefe, where the Scripture is silent, the Church is my Text; where that speakes, 'tis but my Comment; where there is a joynt silence of both, I borrow not the rules of my Religion from Rome or Geneva, but the dictates of my own reason.'[45]

2

The People in the Pews

'The very life of religion consists in practice'
– Robert South

ROBERT SOUTH (1634–1716), who wrote the above words, distinguished himself by declining both the bishopric of Rochester and the Deanery of Westminster in one year. He is critical of what he terms 'a naked, unoperative, faith' which places religion 'in languid, abortive velleities, and so cuts the nerves of all endeavour, by rating glory at a bare desire, and eternity at a wish'.[1]

In other words, he is saying that our religion must cause us to *do* something and to *become* something. It must work on us *externally* and *internally* and be seen to do so. The obvious course therefore is to make some investigation of Anglican practice in the seventeenth century and how better to do that than to consider how the laity of the period went about what St Bernard called 'the business of all businesses', the putting into practice of their religion? We have been looking at the theology and the thinking characteristic of the spirit of Anglicanism and now we are to use the second of our two merging approaches to see what that Anglican ethos produced in practice. What did it look like in action? In essence, Christian theoria and Christian praxis are not to be separated. Yet, though the faith is 'once for all delivered' it evokes a plurality of response, both ecclesial and cultural. So how did Anglicans respond in the seventeenth century?

I have chosen to speak of a doctor, a couple of high civil servants, a man of leisure, a country gentleman who knew everybody and was of noble birth, a scientist, a banker and several devout ladies. Yet, the choice is possible mainly because their lives are recorded by themselves or by those who knew them. If we want to see the whole picture we can never be unmindful of the nameless numbers who, many of them illiterate or barely literate, attended the churches not only on Sundays but often on weekdays as well. One recalls not only George Herbert's poorer neighbours who would let their ploughs rest when they heard his daily bell which, says Izaak Walton, 'brought most of his Parishioners, and many gentlemen in the Neighbourhood, constantly to make a part of his Congregation twice a day'. One remembers also those working men who used to resort with their tools under their arms to the early daily service in St Olave's, Waterford. The records show, in fact, that sizeable congregations appeared at weekday services both in Ireland and England during the period and well on into the early nineteenth century.[2]

Sir Thomas Browne (1605–1682)

The fact that Browne was one of the prosecution witnesses at a witchcraft trial in 1664 and that he could also at the same time allow the possibility of the creation-narrative in Genesis being an allegory tells us much not only about himself but about the transitional society of which he was part: 'For my part I have ever believed, and do now know, that there are witches: they that doubt of these, do not only deny *them*, but Spirits; and are obliquely and upon consequence a sort not of Infidels, but Atheists'.[3] He was not alone in this: Joseph Glanvill, the source of Matthew Arnold's *Scholar Gypsy*, was a forward-looking theologian, an amateur of science and a supporter of the Royal Society who actively sought an alliance between religion and science and an agreement of reason and faith. Yet in his works, such as *Sadducismus Triumphatus* (1667) he too asserts that there are witches. During the century, trials and even torture were frequent in England and still more so in Scotland. New England towards the close of the century was particularly bad. So far as I know there was only one such trial in Ireland, that of Dame Alice Kyteler in fourteenth-century Kilkenny. She escaped but one of her alleged coven Petronilla was flogged and burned. For fifteen years I lived in the Bishop's house built by Richard Ledrede who had instigated the prosecution. Why, we ask, would two highly intelligent men like Browne and Glanvill take this line? The answer I think lies in their awareness of the transitional nature of the times and their anxiety that the new science, which they supported, should not be seen to be inimical to the whole category of the supernatural. It is worth dwelling for a moment on this changing perception of reality because it is the climate in which the author of the *Religio Medici* practised the Christian religion. Browne's is a mind in which Renaissance man has not yet quite come to recognise in himself the last vestiges of the Middle Ages. On the other hand, his contemporary Bishop Wilkins, Cromwell's brother-in-law and an early member of the Royal Society, had progressed further than Browne into what we think of as the modern world. A mathematician and astronomer, he discussed 'the possibility of framing an ark for submarine navigations', the likelihood of having 'a flying chariot' and a telephone. Glanvill too, in his *Scepsis Scientifica*, considers that 'posterity will find many things, that are now but rumours, verified into practical realities' and he visualises lunar travel, flight and 'conferring at the distance of the Indies by sympathetic conveyances may be as usual to future times, as to us in a literary correspondence'. Wilkins also considers that the earth may be a planet, that men may reach the moon and 'that a plurality of worlds doth not contradict any principle of reason or faith'.[4] Scripture is perfect for the purpose for which it was intended and 'matters of faith and religion must be propounded in such a way as to render them highly credible, so as an honest and teachable man may safely assent to them'.[5] Thus he occupies a half-way house between the Cambridge Platonists and the later Latitudinarians, naturalists and scientists. He used a plain style in preaching and was a sound moral theologian and wrote a book on prayer.

This was the changing climate of opinion in which Browne produced his *Religion of a Physician* in a very different style, the rich allusive style shortly to be replaced by the simple lucidity favoured by the Royal Society, but he too showed the same concern for practice in his *Christian Morals* published posthumously in 1716.

His religion is that of a Christian intellectual of his day in a profession 'despite of which I dare without usurpation assume the honourable style of a Christian'.[6] Doctors were not then reckoned as devotees. Browne understood six languages (II.8). He studied medicine at Montpellier and Padua and took his doctorate at Leyden. Although his book was not meant for publication various friends read it in manuscript and a pirated edition appeared in 1642 with the result that when officially published it became widely popular especially among fellow-intellectuals delighted by the seeming paradox of a devout doctor who was a regular worshipper in that superb church, St Peter Mancroft in Norwich.

'It might be said of Browne that he thought with his imagination' and this is both the secret of his charm as a writer and a determinant in the texture of his faith.[7] The *Religio Medici* could be described as comprising two parts, one centring on faith and beliefs and the other on charity and this incidentally matches with our dual approach to the Anglican heritage in this book. It is the religion of a cultivated man who has worked out for himself from his experience and observation what he considers life to be all about: 'The world that I regard is myself'.[8] He is Christian by conviction 'not that I meerly owe this title to the font . . . but having in my riper years and confirmed judgment seen and examined all, I find my self obliged by the principles of grace, and the law of mine own reason, to embrace no other name but this'.[9] He counts his age from his baptism, not 'esteeming my self any thing before I was my Saviours, and inrolled in the register of Christ'.[10] He is a convinced and committed Anglican but his charity towards fellow-Christians of other traditions is as sincere as it was uncommon in his day: 'I could never hear the Ave-Mary Bell without an elevation; or think it a sufficient warrant, because *they* erred in one circumstance, for me to err in all, that is, in silence and dumb contempt'.[11] He agrees that 'there is cause of passion between us' but it is as uncharitable in us to scoff at the Bishop of Rome as it is for 'our adversaries . . . to compute the nativity of our religion from Henry the Eighth'.[12] For himself 'I have no genius to disputes in religion' and in spite of two or three heresies in the days of 'my greener studies' reason and reflection have led him so that now 'in divinity I love to keep the road; and though not in an implicite, yet an humble faith, follow the great wheel of the Church'.[13] The inward gentleness of his religion expresses itself outwardly in a reverence which 'misguided zeal termes superstition . . . at my devotion I love to use the civility of my knee, my hat, and hand, with all those outward and sensible motions, which may express, or promote, my invisible devotion . . . at the sight of a cross or crucifix I can dispence with my hat, but scarce with the thought or memory of my Saviour'.[14] To study Thomas Browne's religion is to be fascinated by the interplay of reason and mystery, of acceptance and questioning in a personality that is as original as it is attractive. He has no time for debating 'airy subtleties in religion' but the mystery of faith absorbs his mind: 'the deepest mysteries ours contains have not only been illustrated, but maintained, by syllogism and the rule of reason. I love to lose myself in a mystery, to pursue my reason to an *O altitudo!* 'Tis my solitary recreation to pose my apprehension with those involved aenigmas and riddles of the Trinity, with Incarnation, and resurrection . . . I desire to exercise my faith in the difficultest point; for to credit ordinary and visible objects is not faith, but persuasion'.[15]

One can see why the book became a best-seller amongst the discerning of the day who were captivated and, I would imagine, helped (as was Sir Kenelm Digby who read it through the night) by the picture of a devout man of parts treading the tight-rope of faith and reason, of mystery, science and natural observation, with a deep and sympathetic perception of the amphibiousness of being human. 'We carry with us the wonders we seek without us: there is all Africa and her prodigies in us'[16] and 'The whole Creation is a mystery, and particularly that of Man'.[17]

The almost irresistible temptation is to go on quoting as one enters further into the mind of one whose individuality expresses itself so engagingly and whose questionings and wistful admissions of occasional incomprehension keep company with the living faith and active devotion of one whose 'desires onely are . . . to be but the last man, and bring up the rere in heaven'.[18] The heart warms to Sir Thomas with his honesty and humility and wry self-recognition: 'This is the tenor of my belief; wherein though there be many things singular, and to the humour of my irregular self, yet, if they square not with maturer judgements, I disclaim them'.[19] Yet the flights of fancy and the curiosity of an enquiring mind, now wondering about the continuation of miracles, now intrigued by the society of bees and ants – 'the civility of these little citizens'[20] – are never allowed to obscure an honest and sensitive religion: 'For my original sin, I hold it to be washed away in my baptism: for my actual transgressions, I compute and reckon with God but from my last repentance, Sacrament, or general absolution; and therefore am not terrified with the sins or madness of my youth'.[21] For him, charity is the heart of religious practice 'without which Faith is a meer notion'[22] and he counts himself fortunate that he has escaped the temptation to pride 'a mortal enemy to Charity, the first and father-sin'.[23] He puts this down not to merit but to his temperament 'for I am of a constitution so general, that it consorts and sympathiseth with all things'. Browne is blessed with an inherited contentment of disposition and an acceptance of others and of circumstances – 'I have no antipathy . . . in any thing'.[24] His charity stems from an awareness of his own needs and the conviction that to give to the poor is to lend to the Lord: 'upon this motive only I cannot behold a beggar without relieving his necessities with my purse or his soul with my prayers'.[25] The whole person is his concern. 'I cannot goe to cure the body of my patient, but I forget my profession, and call unto God for his soule'(II.6). He is in fact a profoundly sympathetic but not a sentimental character. 'Acquaint thyself with the physiognomy of want' he writes in *Christian Morals* and 'spare not where thou canst not easily be prodigal'.[26] The man who could spin words with such a delicacy of insight took his own advice in practice: 'Be a moralist of the Mount . . . and christianize Thy Notions'.[27] The delightfully aphoristic style ('be chast in thy flaming days')[28] cloaks but does not conceal a plain and direct moral theology – 'Live by old ethicks and the classical rules of honesty'[29] – nor reduce spirituality to moralism – 'Have a glimpse of incomprehensibles, and thoughts of things, which thoughts but tenderly touch'.[30] Here is a practising Christian, a physician and an intellectual of what he calls 'this strict enquiring age' who encourages his reader to 'let thy studies be free . . . joyn sense unto reason, and experiment unto speculation'.[31] Yet all the time the world invisible he views, the world intangible he touches: 'Since there is something of us that will still live on, join both lives together, and live in one but for the other . . . and if . . . any have been so happy as personally to understand Christian annihilation, extasy, exolution, transformation, the kiss of the Spouse, and ingression into the Divine Shadow, according to mystical theology, they have already had an handsome anticipation of Heaven'.[32] We cannot take leave of this uncommon fellow-member of the household of faith without recording that for Browne prayer 'is the dormative I take to bedward'. No sleeping pills are needed by one who closes 'mine eyes in security . . . and sleep unto the Resurrection'[33]

Small wonder that the diarist John Evelyn 'was not hardly perswaded' to make the rough run to Norwich with Lord Henry Howard 'in his flying Charriat with 6 horses' on the spur of the moment: 'having a desire to see that famous scholar and physition Dr T. Browne author of *Religio Medici* . . . and now lately knighted'. He was charmed by Browne – they had corresponded but never met – 'The whole house and garden being a Paradise and Cabinet of rarities' and Evelyn fell in love with Norwich.[34]

James Bonnell (1653–1699)

The Norwich connection is maintained in our next layman who lived out his Anglicanism across the Irish Sea in seventeenth-century Dublin. He was a top civil servant, Accountant

General of Ireland, and of such known probity that even 'during the late King James's reign . . . they never thought of removing him from his employment . . . and the enemies of his religion reverenced his person'.[35] So wrote his biographer, William Hamilton, who knew Bonnell and gathered his material from the Accountant General's many friends, including various bishops who contributed commendatory notes. Yet, as Hamilton notes, his chief advantage in this effort to picture real religion 'not in notion but in life' was not only 'the large memorials of his life put into my hands, drawn up by his most intimate friends, both in England and Ireland'. 'The principal materials for Mr Bonnell's Life are his own private papers . . . what he himself calls them, the transcript of his heart'.[36] These are chiefly meditations and prayers composed by Bonnell, often on returning from Holy Communion. The reader cannot but be deeply impressed by the Christian life revealed in all this first-hand evidence of friends and personal writings which he feels secures him from the well-meant excesses of hagiography. Hamilton is aware that those who did not know Bonnell might think that the *Life* 'runs too much in the strain of panegyric and commendation'. On the contrary, he insists, to have known Bonnell and to read what he wrote, is to realize that the biography is the true story of a saintly layman. Indeed, Bonnell's friend, Bishop Wetenhall wrote 'I am truly of the opinion that, in the best age of the Church, had he lived therein, he would have passed for a saint'.[37] But we must not think in terms of stained glass and haloes: 'Here we have an instance of one who reconciled a life of religion and business together'.[38] Bishop King spoke of 'the peculiar charms and graces that almost ravished those that conversed with him'. He was 'tall, well-shaped and fair. His aspect was comely and showed great sweetness mixed with life and sprightliness'. People were aware of his ease of manner and cheerfulness. He was approachable and understanding, not judgmental: 'none made greater allowance for human nature'.[39] The mainspring of all was his religious belief and practice. Another bishop and friend described him as 'a true son of the Established Church, and a most exact observer of her rules and offices: he was also exceedingly charitable to the poor and always zealous in the promotion of piety'.[40] His biographer wrote 'Must it not also be matter of great joy to the Church of England to see all its principles and laws so truly transcribed in the life of one of its excellent sons' and that indeed is my theme here, for Bonnell lived out in daily practice the Christian faith as this Church has received it.

Before we take a closer look at how he practised his religion externally and internally, I would clarify with a few biographical particulars my reference to the Norwich connection.Born in Genoa in 1653, he was the son of Samuel Bonnell a merchant trading out of Leghorn but who moved to England in 1655 with his wife, Rebecca Sayer of Norwich. The connection is a double one because Bonnell's great grandfather, a native of Ypres, who had fled from Alba's persecution of the Protestants in the Low Countries, settled in Norwich where he was 'afterwards chosen Mayor of that city'. We recall that the author of *The Religion of a Physician* had also settled in Norwich in 1636–7 just as did the forbears of Bonnell whose *Life* might well have been entitled *The Religion of a Layman*. He was sent to the Diocesan School at Trim, Co. Meath and then to a private school in Oxfordshire. At Cambridge, his tutor was Calamy and already he was adopting a rule of life, keeping the Church's fasts but concealing the fact from his college room-mate. After degree, he did some tutoring on the Continent during which he courageously nursed his pupil through the smallpox. In 1684, Bonnell returned to Ireland to take up work as Accountant General and people soon found that he was totally to be trusted and not for sale. 'Three pieces of broad gold' left on his table as a sweetener were given to old retired customs officers. At this time, high civil servants like Pepys and his colleagues took this as a matter of course, as we learn from the *Diary*, looking to double their income from such judicious gratuities from contractors to the Navy Yard. Bonnell was quite different: 'He never knew what gratuity or reward meant, confining his gains entirely to his salary'.[41] A giver, not a taker, says Hamilton 'by the exactest computation his intimate friends could make . . . he gave away the eighth part of his yearly income to the poor'.[42] He was courageous too and refused to take flight to England in 1688 when a massacre of Protestants was rumoured. When the Anglican churches were turned into prisons and the clergy were confined he accounted this a judgment for the neglect of worship as he noted in a prayer composed a few days before the decisive Battle of the Boyne in 1690 when the Williamite forces were victorious.

Bonnell's was a religion of commitment to Christ in the Church's Way, a religion of 'inward' expressing itself through 'outward' and of 'outward' vivified (the word is St Bernard's)[43] by 'inward'. Central to it was the dynamic of rule, of daily church-going, of weekly sacrament, of private prayer and meditation – all expressed in charity, humility, recollection and self-discipline, in the service of God and the neighbour. His religion was the authentic article and inevitably attracted and influenced others. No matter how heavy the pressures of work he went to church twice a day 'and when the hurry of his business hindered this . . . he would use all his art to get prayers at some church or other'.[44] This presented no difficulty as the daily services were widely available and used in the Church of Ireland during the period and this was noted by the former Jesuit, Andrew Sall.[45] Nor was this confined to the cities as a rural curate like Philip Skelton looked to have 30 or 40 at daily prayers in Monaghan.[46] One recalls the founder of the Dublin banking dynasty, David La Touche, going from the bank every day to Mattins in the Castle chapel until 1745, when he collapsed at service and died. This aspect of Anglican practice amongst the laity continued on and in 1821 there was daily service 'in every church in Dublin and many were well attended.'[47] This was the practice which provided the outward framework of Bonnell's religion and most important for him was the weekly eucharist at which, if he had to go to a front seat, he would shorten his private prayers 'that he might not be taken notice of'.[48]

The influences on Bonnell's faith and practice were, primarily, the Scriptures 'his constant and daily study', the liturgy and Lewis Bayly's *The Practice of Piety*. This was a widely popular book and he tells us that it led him to 'the proposal of a methodical course of religion'.⁴⁹ This he faithfully discharged, beginning each day with prayer 'in his closet' and each evening repeating the *Magnificat* before self-examination and meditation. His papers preserve prayers for use at bed-time, at lying down, at waking, at getting out of bed, at washing and at kneeling in the day-time.⁵⁰ This is in the direct tradition of the many Anglican books of devotion such as Jeremy Taylor's *Holy Living* but Bonnell had other favourites too. Hamilton records that 'all books of devotion he read with a very sensible pleasure' and these included *The Imitation of Christ* and Francis de Sales' *Introduction to a Devout Life* (1613) of which Bonnell made a translation.

The eucharist was the subject of 'a great part of his private writings'. 'He was very early touched with a lively sense of his obligation to commemorate our Saviour's Passion in that Holy Mystery'⁵¹ says Hamilton who notes that even at the age of fourteen James had objected to the infrequency of communion at his private school in Oxfordshire. His eucharistic writings are rich in devotion 'to every part of our Saviour's bitter Passion' which he relates to the transforming of the Christian's experience. For him, the eucharist is a life-changing mystery: 'My Saviour impregnated the consecrated elements and in a manner embodied himself there; yet still remaining where he was, filling heaven and earth but more particularly our chancel: saying to us: You are all my friends and worthy, whatever your sins be, through my sufferings'. The eucharist is 'immortal love wrapt up in bread'. 'The glorious bread 'and the communicant's faith concur in renewing the life and practice of the members of Christ's Family. The Presence is real, the gift of the Spirit, but it must be apprehended: 'The Holy Elements are impregnated with the materials of life, like the first framing of a living creature or embryo before it is quickened. But they are quickened with spiritual life only upon the faith of each receiver which God hath appointed to be the concurring instrument or means of this divine quickening'.⁵² The Presence is really given, Christ has 'impregnated the consecrated elements' and has 'embodied himself there', through the Spirit. Faith does not create the Presence but apprehends, and appropriates it as a 'concurring instrument'. The Presence and the faith are both the work of the Spirit and are inseparable in the whole eucharistic action. As ARCIC I put it 'When this offering is met by faith, a lifegiving encounter results'.[53]

We are looking then at a deeply devotional religion in which the internal aspect results through its perfect balance with the outward aspect of practice in a life of striking spiritual maturity. Hamilton depicts it as a growth in the key-virtues of humility and charity, in temperance, chastity and justice, and in prayer. Each is illustrated by Bonnell's own meditations on the subject. His goal was 'poor in heart, pure in heart and lowly in heart' after the pattern of the humility of Christ, 'Him whom he so dearly loved'.[54] Here in fact and action are being worked out those principles of moral-ascetic theology which were the hall-mark of Anglican spirituality in the seventeenth century. Here is a life, all too short, of a great beauty which drew others and convinced them that religion really works. 'It was a piety' writes F. R. Bolton 'we have seen exemplified . . . in the lives of James Duke of Ormonde and the Lord Lieutenants of Caroline times, of noblemen and private families, of James Bonnell and busy officials, of young men in the city of Dublin, and Waterford working-men who went to early prayers with their tools under their arms'.[55]

Sadly, Bonnell died 'of a malignant fever' at the early age of forty-six to the grief of his wife who shared to the full his religious outlook on life, and to the distress of friends in all walks of life, not least 'the poor and necessitous whom he studied to comfort and relieve'.[56] Bonnell was a cultivated man, well-versed in the classics, a French speaker and a student of Hebrew. He studied the Fathers and left a translation of part of Synesius in his papers. Like his fellow civil servant Pepys, he was an amateur of music and mathematics. His Anglicanism was intellectually as well as devotionally based on the appeal to Scripture, antiquity and reason. He records his admiration of Hooker, the great exponent of this appeal, 'whom he used to commend as an author who writ with a primitive spirit but modern judgment and correctness'. He comments approvingly on the 'primitive' nature of the Church of England and he frequently uses the word 'rational' of devotion in which a markedly affective quality can also be discerned: 'he saw her constitution primitive and apostolical; her doctrine, pure; her service, rational and heavenly . . . he had the justest value and highest veneration for that great repository of true devotion, the Liturgy of our Church'.[57] As might be expected from the quality of Bonnell's spirituality, while 'he was zealous for the Church' . . . he was 'yet charitable to those who differed from him'. Typically, 'the divisions which prevail among Christians he heartily bewailed'.[58]

Samuel Pepys (1633–1703)

I have mentioned Pepys and I think that a comment on his religious practice may help to round out the picture. Bonnell's contemporary and fellow civil servant, he was a very different character although they had in common business ability, interest in music and mathematics, in books and intellectual pursuits. To him we owe so vivid a delineation of his life and times that the sights, sounds and smells of seventeenth-century London as well as the greater events of the day are made real for us. The immense value of the *Diary* is obvious to us all but what requires noting in the context of our investigation is the nature of his practice as an Anglican. We all know the delightful mistranslation of 'Non Angli, sed Angeli' – 'not angels, but Anglicans'. Not all Anglicans are angels and Pepys certainly was not. A frequent churchgoer he was also aware of the charms of female members of the congregation. He had been brought up under puritan influences and disapproved of gambling and bad language but his private life shows reaction against his early background. His criticism of the King having mistresses he apparently did not apply to himself. A loyal member of the Church of England, he was against Roman Catholicism, but not fanatically so, and he favoured toleration and approved proposals for unity between the Presbyterians and the Anglicans. One cannot do better than close this comment (made, so to speak, to redress the balance of the picture) with an extract from the introduction to the splendid 1970 edition of the *Diary* by one of the chief editors, Robert Latham. He writes 'We are more interested in a man's politics or religion if we know what he had for dinner. To the historian, one of the most interesting features of these private and domestic revelations is perhaps the information they give about Pepys's religion – *to many of Pepys's contemporaries the most vital of all issues* – his ecclesiastical position, clear enough by the time the diary opens, was by then that of a middle-of-the-road Erastian, distrustful of both ritualists and precisians, a loyal son of the Church of England but a strong critic of its clergy . . . After the Restoration he went to his parish church with respectable frequency rather than with devout regularity; and if he slept during the sermon he usually had the excuse that it was during the afternoon service. In the whole of the diary period, he apparently never made his communion,. . . His Lents were kept sketchily, and he observed Sunday as best he could, which was sometimes not very well. He read his Bible only a little, and (probably in common with many other householders) regarded family prayers mainly as a method of household management. He was at bottom, in the diary period, a worldling. Yet there can be no doubt of the sincerity of his religious feelings. He turned naturally to God, when alone, to express thanks or to ask for protection and help. His Anglicanism may have been loosely formulated in so far as it was a creed, but as a social discipline it was a cause to which his loyalty was firm'.

Interestingly and confirmatory of the picture being developed here, Latham remarks '*Perhaps he was less religious than most men of his class and generation*, but his views on toleration – or something like them – were widespread among the educated laity, and it was on ecclesiastical pragmatism of this sort – *on the layman's common sense* – that the solutions of these problems reached at the Revolution of 1688–9 were largely to rest'.[59]

We shall see whether a further examination of the religion of the laity supports our assessment.

3
More People in the Pews

'The very life of religion consists in practice'
– Robert South

IN my possession I have a tiny pocket edition of Izaak Walton's *The Compleat Angler*, bound in black and resembling a small prayer book. It used to belong to my father, a keen fisherman who in his later years became very deaf and was accustomed to read *The Compleat Angler* during the sermon which he was unable to hear. Thus, unintentionally he acquired an adventitious reputation for piety. He could have done worse and, given the circumstances, could hardly have done better because the book with its May morning charm is a gentle and thoughtful book. It is a Christian book reflecting the religious balance and the devout Anglicanism of its author.

Izaak Walton (1593–1683)

Walton, whose father kept a pub, was all his life a staunch Royalist and a devoted Anglican. He became a draper by trade in London, having his place of business in Fleet Street and being an active parishioner of the church of St Dunstan's-in-the-West. He did not conceal either his religion or his politics during the Commonwealth and he appears to have left London for Stafford, possibly (says Margaret Bottrall) because of his 'outspoken sympathies'.[1] He did well in business and was twice married, first to Rachel Floud, a niece of one of Richard Hooker's favourite pupils and a descendant of Archbishop Cranmer's brother. She died in 1640 after fourteen years of marriage and none of their seven children survived infancy. Six years later, Walton married Anne Ken, half-sister to Thomas Ken the famous bishop and hymn-writer. Who does not know

33

'Awake my soul, and with the Sun / Thy daily stage of Duty run' and 'Glory to Thee my God, this night / For all the blessings of the Light'? Who does not recall that Charles II, clear-sighted enough to recognize the genuine article when he saw it, was generous enough to consider for promotion 'the little fellow who refused poor Nelly a lodging'.[2] Walton's Anglican credentials were therefore unimpeachable but it was for himself that he was valued by contemporaries and by posterity. This layman's contribution to the Anglican heritage was the modesty of an unassuming personal devotion which expressed itself in the quality of his own life and in the *Lives* he wrote of *John Donne* (1640), *Sir Henry Wotton* (1651), *Richard Hooker* (1662), *George Herbert* (1670) and *Robert Sanderson* (1678). He worked at a *Life* of John Hales but never completed it.

Walton knew personally the poets Donne and King, the theologian John Hales, and many of the clergy of the day particularly Bishop George Morley to whom he acted as steward in the dioceses of Worcester and Winchester. Whether one values more the *Lives* or *The Compleat Angler* depends no doubt on one's personal preferences but if one is both an Anglican and a fisherman one can value them equally. The *Lives* are small masterpieces and though they contain inaccuracies they convey a sensitive understanding of the men who are their subjects and a deep and loving appreciation of the Church which they served and of its way of devotion, discipline and duty. 'Somehow, somewhere', wrote Margaret Bottrall 'this London draper, the son of a Staffordshire ale-house-keeper, acquired a love of books, an interest in the as yet undeveloped art of biography, and the ability to use the English language for the pleasure and profit of innumerable readers'.[3] It even surprised Izaak Walton himself as he says in one of his prefaces to the *Lives* 'When I sometime look back upon my education and mean abilities, 'tis not without some little wonder at myself that I am come to be publicly in print'.

Yet undoubtedly he has an art of recreating the atmosphere of a place and of communicating something of the reality of a person though as through a veil woven both of memory and imagination. It is always May morning in *The Compleat Angler*.

Whether Piscator is enlarging on the subject of maggots and worms for bait, or noting that the first apostles called were fishermen, or recording that men like Dean Nowell, George Herbert, Sir Henry Wotton and Perkins were all 'brethren of the Angle', there is a vernal innocence about the book which is most endearing. One somehow senses that this is reality at one remove, almost a fairyland but the fairyland of a Christian. Venator might well have included Walton among 'those primitive Christians that you love'.[4] Charles Cotton, whose Supplement is bound with *The Compleat Angler* in my small copy, calls him 'my father Walton' and adds that 'he likes none but such as he believes to be very honest men' and 'I must tell you further, that I have the happiness to know his person, and to be intimately acquainted with him, and in him to know the worthiest man, and to enjoy the best and the truest friend any man ever had'. It seems to be the general impression he made on contemporaries – 'honest Izaak', 'the trusty hand of Mr Izaak Walton'. As one attempts an evaluation at second hand across the centuries, one concludes that he was one of those whose simple goodness is so transparent that it just did not occur to any of his acquaintance to think of questioning it. No doubt as a historian he has limitations and as a biographer some slight tendency to hagiography, but love and gentleness and deep religious feeling and a taste for life's simple pleasures all come through in his writing. He knew and consorted with men of importance in his day but such friendships and associations never went to his head who was always ready to 'lay aside business' and to go 'a-fishing with honest Nat. and R. Roe'.[5] Walton died at the age of ninety and was buried in Winchester Cathedral where he would often have joined in the worship of what he calls 'our good old Service-book' which he praises more than once in *The Compleat Angler*.[6]

The Hon. Robert Boyle (1627–1691)

We turn next from the son of a tavern-keeper to the son of the richest subject of the Crown in his day. The Hon. Robert

Boyle, scientist and linguist, a younger son of the Earl of Cork was born at Lismore Castle which still stands impressively above the River Blackwater as it flows through Co. Waterford. The Earl was vastly wealthy and Robert was born into a class whose connections ensured easy access to the learned men of his day and whose material possessions made it possible for him to engage in the research which made him famous. Known to us as the discoverer of 'Boyle's law', the son of the Lord High Treasurer of Ireland became so famous in his own right as a scientist that no distinguished visitor to England felt that his trip was complete unless he could meet Boyle. Roger Pilkington has dubbed him 'the Father of Chemistry' because there was no aspect of science which was not in some measure indebted to the modest and retiring scholar who set up his laboratory at Oxford in 1654.[7] Today when Boyle's name crops up so do vague thoughts of science and experiments 'touching the Spring of the Air'. What is forgotten, or not known, is that Boyle's approach to science was religious through and through. This comes across in all his works and moderns are surprised to learn that he was as active in the Corporation for the Spread of the Gospel in New England as he was in the Royal Society. He was for moderation and tolerance in religion and practised what he believed, helping ejected Welsh non-conformist ministers out of his own pocket. A committed Anglican, he saw God as revealed both in the natural world and in the Scriptures. In *The Christian Virtuoso* (1690) he maintained the thesis that experimental philosophy – science – helped rather than hindered a man from being 'a good Christian'. In the same way, he studied Oriental languages to obtain a greater understanding of the Bible. There are two books which proclaim the wisdom and the love of God – the book of nature and the Scriptures. This was the theme of his contemporaries like Ray, the naturalist, Wilkins the imaginative natural theologian, Willughby and others. They knew one another and the whole thrust of the 'new philosophy' was influencing not only the theologians but the thinking public. Pepys read 'Mr. Boyle's book of Colours' as he was rowed up the Thames. The perception of reality was changing and the vocation of men like Boyle was to ensure that the new science would be seen as strengthening rather than weakening Christian faith and practice. He even saw this as a particular ministry for the educated laity. There is a sentence of his which says this clearly: 'Yet, it cannot well be denied, but that if all other circumstances be equal, he is the fittest to commend divinity, whose profession it is not'. This comes from the preface to his '*The Excellency of Theology compar'd with Natural Philosophy*' which was written in 1665 when Boyle was living in the country to avoid the plague. It was published in 1674. The sentence crystallizes Boyle's thoughts on the calling and duties of a member of the Church, especially one whose circumstances gave him time, freedom and independence. Thus, with Bonnell, Boyle and others, the lay-theologian made an early appearance in Anglicanism. If Browne gave us '*The Religion of a Physician*' and Bonnell demonstrated '*The Religion of a Layman*', Boyle's life and work together constituted *The Religion of a Scientist*. His book on *The Usefulness of Experimental Natural Philosophy* (1663) was a reassuring publication for educated contemporaries who saw that the new philosophy could go hand in hand with practising membership of the Church. Boyle, Wilkins and Ray helped to create for this view a favourable atmosphere and climate of opinion in their generation.

As a boy, Robert was sent to Eton and then, with his brother Francis spent some years in Geneva in the care of a tutor named Marcombes. During his time there he had intellectual difficulties about religion. In the course of a violent storm he had a religious experience as a result of which he decided for a deliberate change, that 'he might not owe his more deliberate consecration of himself to piety to any less noble motive than that of its own excellence'. Thomas Birch, the first editor of Boyle's works, tells us something of this experience in *The Life of the Honourable Robert Boyle* and it appears that the young intellectual was still unable to accept the full Christian understanding that the God he now accepted could also be the God who revealed Himself in Christ. 'Christ crucified – to the Greeks foolishness' – that was the stumbling block. He went regularly to church but abstained from the Sacrament. Pilkington's account of Boyle's second and final conversion is moving: 'Then one day the unexpected happened. For no particular reason – other than desperation – Robert entered a church and accepted the Sacrament. And at the same moment his world was transformed, for 'at last it pleased God to restore unto him the withdrawn sense of his favour'. From that day onward he experienced a sense of reconciliation and restored faith which was never to leave him'.[8]

Robert was never to see his father again as the Earl died in 1643 towards the end of the war in Ireland which temporarily brought to an end the family prosperity. Boyle went to live in London with his sister Katharine, deserted by her husband Viscount Ranelagh. He then went to visit his property at Stalbridge in Dorset where he began his study of chemistry. He settled here for six years as the Civil War dragged on and his close relationship with his devoted sister who kept house for him for thirty-three years gave him the support he needed. Boyle never really knew his mother and he never married. As the years passed, Katharine's house in Pall Mall became the centre to which resorted the theologians, the scientists and the many visitors from the Continent.[9] Boyle dedicated many of his works to her and she was the 'Sophronia' of his *Reflections*. It was recorded of her (and here we see another example of the religious quality of the age at its best) that 'She was contented with what she had, and though she was twice stript of it she never moved on her own account, but was the general intercessor for all persons of merit or in want . . . she divided her charities and friendships, her esteem as well as her bounty, with the truest regard to merit . . . without any difference made upon the account of opinion. She had . . . a vast reach of knowledge . . . and the deepest sense of religion . . . that was known perhaps in that age'.[10] She acted as a spiritual counsellor to Hyde, Earl of Clarendon, who was appointed Lord High Chancellor by Charles II while still in exile.

Brother and sister, so alike in temperament and outlook on

life, shared their religion also, beginning every day with prayer and meditation together. Boyle's religion was deep-based, tolerant and all-pervasive. His conviction was intellectual as well as spiritual and appears in his scientific works as much as in his *Considerations touching the Style of the Holy Scriptures* or his *Excellency of Theology*. His *Occasional Reflections*, regarded now as more or less charming moralisings, were practically a best seller in their day but were mocked by Jonathan Swift in his *Pious Meditation on a Broom Staff*. Boyle's objective was 'to make the world vocal' by using ordinary things so as 'to make the world both a library and an oratory'.[11] He himself regarded them as 'trifles' and it was Katharine who persuaded him to publish them. Like everyone at the time he must have known the *Religio Medici* and while Browne and Boyle had a shared approach to natural studies and theology seeing them as complementary, Boyle was a scientist in the full meaning of the term while Browne was a gifted amateur and enquirer. The *Reflections* are stilted compared to the magic of the *Religio Medici*'s style but it has always seemed to me that Browne's book must have been a part inspiration for Boyle's reflections. I find a marked verbal resemblance between this sentence from the *Religio Medici*: 'Surely the heathens knew better how to join and read these mystical letters than we Christians, who cast a more careless eye on these common hieroglyphics, and disdain to suck divinity from the flowers of nature' and this from the *Reflections*: 'the creatures are the true Egyptian hieroglyphics, that under the rude forms of birds and beasts conceal the mysterious secrets of knowledge and piety'.[12]

At the age of sixty-four the great scientist died one week after the death of Katharine. His health was never robust but his spirit was strong in self-dedication, in modesty despite his renown, and in the humility which caused him to refuse a peerage at the Restoration. To see someone through the eyes of a contemporary is as near as we can ever come to bridging the centuries. If the eyes are those of a friend of forty years' standing then we feel that we can in part pierce time's defenses. Happily for posterity, that friend was John Evelyn and his *Diary* records constant visits over the years to Boyle and many scientific discussions for Evelyn too was a member of the Royal Society of which his illustrious friend was President. What a party it must have been one day in 1656 when 'Mr Rob: Boyle that excellent person and greate *Virtuoso*, Dr Jeremy Taylor and Dr Wilkins dined with me at *Sayes Court*', Evelyn's country residence.[13] Evelyn was a trustee for Boyle's numerous charitable bequests and he was at the funeral of 'that pious admirable Christian, excellent philosopher, and my worthy friend Mr Boyle, a greate losse to the publique'. He records a summary of the sermon preached by Gilbert Burnet, Bishop of Salisbury: 'Mr Boyle, who made God and Religion the object and scope of all his excellent tallents in the knowledge of Nature, who had arrived to so high a degree in it, accompanied with such zeale and extraordinary piety . . . *the exact life he led*, and the happy end which he made . . . and truly all this was but his due, without any grain of flattery . . . not onely England, but all the learned world suffered a publique losse in this greate and good man, and my particular worthy friend'.[14]

John Evelyn (1620–1706)

Perhaps no other literary form does more to bring to life the realities and the quality of living in other times than does the diary, especially if it was not intended for publication. We think of the diary of Pepys to which Evelyn's diary is a perfect counter-balance. They frequently met and knew each other well enough for Pepys to show Evelyn the stone taken from his bladder – a dangerous and painful operation for which Pepys held a thanksgiving every year. It was a grim business without anaesthetics and Evelyn's account of such an operation which he witnessed in Paris brings vividly before us a frightening aspect of seventeenth-century life. We think too of the Kilvert diary which captures rural life in mid-Victorian England and Wales as in a series of fascinating still-shots. The Woodforde diary and the Armstrong diary reveal the homely details of rectory life in Norfolk in the eighteenth and nineteenth centuries respectively. When, as in Evelyn's case, the diarist knew everyone that mattered in his day we are being presented with an inside commentary on the society of the second tumultuous half of the seventeenth century. When the diarist is a devout and devoted Anglican whose commitment to his Church was constant in foul weather as in fair, we have an unrivalled opportunity of seeing something of how the Anglican ethos expressed itself in practice.

Evelyn came of wealthy and very well-connected stock, the second son of Richard Evelyn of Wotton, Surrey. It was a widespread family, including a couple of baronets and deputy-lieutenants of Surrey in its number. John Evelyn became a student at the Middle Temple in 1637 and went up to Oxford as a fellow-commoner at Balliol but did not reside. The upheaval of the Civil War found him joining the King's Army in 1642 'but was not permitted to stay longer than the 15th (November) by reason of the Army's marching to Glocester, which had left both me and my Brothers exposed to ruine, without any advantage to his Majestie'.[15] Shortly afterwards with the King's approval he left for France and for several years he was travelling on the Continent and paying visits to England when that was possible for a known Royalist. His accounts of his travels which took him to Paris, Geneva, Rome, Naples, Venice, Verona and Milan give fascinating insights into life in these countries. Evelyn had the *entrée* wherever he went and saw the Pope 'blessing of golden roses' and was presented to him. In Rome he heard all 'the most famous preachers' but was put off by the popular superstition which he encountered.[16] In 1647, he was married to the daughter of Sir Richard Browne, baronet, the king's Resident in Paris from whose Embassy Chapel and its worship the exiled Anglicans driven from home by the Cromwellians and exposed in France to heavy proselytism were wont to argue for the visibility and continuance of the Church of England: 'our divines used to argue for the visibility of the Church from his Chapell and Congregation'.[17]

Constantly, wherever he was, John Evelyn practised as a loyal and devout Anglican. Without number are the entries in the *Diary*: 'The Holy Communion followed . . .'; 'I received the holy sacrament'; 'I received the B. Sacrament'; 'the holy sacrament followed'; 'I received the B. Comm. in our Chapell' (i.e. in Paris); 'he gave us the Blessed Sacrament . . . in our parlor . . . which was now wholy out of use in the parish churches which the Presbyterans and Fanatics had usurped'. Clearly, the eucharist is central to his devotion but he went to two services normally each Sunday and one constantly comes upon comments such as 'Mr Wye preached exceedingly well', 'Mr Griffith preached very poetically and floridly', 'the new curate, a pretty hopeful young man, yet somewhat raw, and newly come from the Colledge, full of latine sentences etc., which in time will wear off'. Frequently, after recording reception of the Sacrament we meet little arrow-prayers like 'The Lord Jesus make me thankful', 'O Lord accept me', 'praising him for the opportunity of receiving the Cup of Salvation', and so on. One thing he shared with Pepys whom he knew and for whom he had a high regard was a tendency as he grew older to sleep during the sermon at Evensong: 'slumber exceedingly surprised me'; 'I was very drowsy'.

In 1647 he managed to visit England and got to Hampton Court 'where I had the honour to kisse his Majestie's hand, and give him account of several things I had in charge, he being now in the power of those execrable villains who not long after murder'd him'.[18] He also contrived to get 'privately into the Councill of the rebell Army at Whitehall, where I heard horrid villanies'.[19] In the following January, 1649, Evelyn was again in London and heard Peters and Bradshaw 'inciting the Rebell powers . . . to destroy his Majestie'. On the 30th, Charles I was beheaded and to Evelyn who could not bear to witness the act this was a death for the Faith: 'I kept the day of his *Martyrdom* a fast, and would not be present, at that execrable wickedness'.[20]

During his time in Paris, he was assiduous in attendance at the Embassy Chapel and was present at an ordination of two priests there by the exiled Bishop of Galloway 'in a time of the poor Church of England's affliction'. He was alive to the danger of the episcopate dying out through the deaths of the surviving bishops: 'there being so few Bishops left in England and consequently danger of a faileur of both functions'.[21] Indeed, Hyde, Earl of Clarendon, felt the matter to be so pressing that in 1655 he tried to make arrangements secretly for episcopal consecrations.[22] Throughout this period Evelyn was in touch with the exiled Court, with nobility and gentry, and dispossessed clergy like Cosin and others, many of whom were in very poor circumstances. Archbishop Bramhall was a wanderer and so short of money that he had to act as an auctioneer of captured cargoes in Flushing. Yet in those poverty-stricken years he contrived to write seven books in defence of Anglicanism. He spoke for others as for himself when he wrote that people 'do little imagine with what difficulties poor exiles struggle, whose minds are more intent on what they should eat tomorrow, than what they should write, being chased as vagabonds into the merciless world to beg relief of strangers'.[23] Yet the Lord permitted him to restore the Irish episcopate by consecrating twelve bishops in January 1661 in St Patrick's Cathedral, Dublin. Evelyn was also 'threatened' for the very royalist preface to his translation of La Mothe Le Vayer in *Liberty and Servitude*. All the time, the exiles were deeply concerned for the Anglican heritage: 'Was kept a solemn fast, for the Calamities of our poore Church, now trampl'd on by the Rebells'.[24]

In 1652 he decided to return to England, not before he paid the fare for an ejected Fellow of King's College, Cambridge 'who came miserable to Paris . . . I also clad and provided for him'.[25] Arrived home, he managed to make arrangements to settle down at Sayes Court, Deptford (his father-in-law's property); 'by the advise, and favour of my friends, I was advis'd to reside in it, and compound with the Souldiers; being besides, authoriz'd by his Majestie so to do . . . I had also addresses, and Cyfers, to correspond with his Majestie and Ministers abroad; upon all which inducements, I was persuaded to settle henceforth in England'.[26]

Apart from this, which for Evelyn was more cloak than dagger, he lived quietly at Sayes Court until the Restoration, occupying himself with gardening, study and the deepening of friendships with such as Boyle and Wilkins. During this time the Church of England was virtually proscribed and Evelyn's children were baptized privately at Sayes Court 'according to the rite of the Church of England'.[27] One of these christenings was performed by Jeremy Taylor who had become a close friend and who from that year onwards was Evelyn's spiritual director: 'using him thenceforward as my ghostly father'.[28] They were in frequent correspondence which contains many references to the persecution for their religion suffered by both, chiefly by Taylor who was twice imprisoned. Evelyn took every opportunity to hear his friend preach often at illegally-held Anglican services in the capital. On one occasion when Evelyn was worshipping in London the chapel was surrounded by soldiers who 'held their muskets against us as we came up to receive the Sacred Elements as if they would have shot us at the Altar'. Mostly these services were held in private houses as on Christmas Day 1656, 'at Dr Wild's lodging where I rejoiced to find so full an assembly of devout and sober Christians . . . but I was not able to come so neere the doore for the presse . . . I received the Blessed Sacrament'.[29] The previous Easter he had communicated at St. Gregory's in London, 'The ruling powers conniving at the use of the Liturgie etc. in this church alone'.[30] Such were the difficulties and dangers of being a practising Anglican in that time and place.

After the Restoration in 1660, Evelyn was much in favour at Court though he was repelled by its profligacy. He was appointed to some government commissions and typically, when member of one of them, he stayed on in London to attend to his duties when his fellow-commissioners were frightened from their posts by the plague. When James II acceded he favoured Evelyn who nevertheless was greatly alarmed by the King's antagonism to the Church of England. He witnessed the imprisonment of the seven bishops for refusing to read the Royal Declaration in 1688: 'Wonderful was the concerne of the people for them, infinite crowds of people on their knees, begging their blessing and praying for them as they passed out of the Barge; along the Tower wharfe'.[31] Evelyn accepted the arrival of William of Orange as being the best solution for the Church and the nation. It is tempting to follow his story until he died at the ripe age of 86 but we must conclude. To the end of his days he continued a disciplined devotional life, mainly worshipping at his parish church but frequently going to church in London when his affairs brought him there. 'I went to London' and heard Tenison preach at St. Martin's 'after which the Communion was celebrated to neere 1000 devout people'.[32] He is in constant touch with peers and government ministers and the Archbishop of Canterbury and other bishops but he does not neglect his friendship with Pepys and Boyle and his colleagues of the Royal Society, the presidency of which he declined. It has been written of him that 'his domestic life was pure and his affections strong, and he devoted himself to work of public utility . . . a pious and devoted member of the Church of England'.[33] The last words of the diary are 'Let every one that names the L. Jesus depart from evill, and increase in love of that profession'.

Robert Nelson (1656–1715)

It is not that these seventeenth-century Anglicans knew nothing but Anglicanism. Browne, Bonnell, Boyle and Evelyn had travelled widely and lived abroad, witnessing the worship of other Christians and often worshipping with them, and generally regarding them with charity in a polemical age. Yet they remained solidly Anglican by choice and conviction often bringing others into the Church by their example, as did Evelyn and Boyle.

Robert Nelson, son of 'a considerable Turkey merchant' was such a well-travelled Anglican who spent some years in the small wasteland of the Nonjuring schism. Yet his *Companion for the Festivals and Fasts of the Church of England* (1704) became one of the most popular handbooks of Anglican devotion, 10,000 copies being printed in four and a half years and reaching thirty-six editions by the beginning of the last century. My copy is the twenty-first edition (1757). The

Companion witnesses to the enormous devotional importance of the *Book of Common Prayer* which has been described as the matrix of Anglican spirituality.[34] A similar book with a similar title *A Companion to the Temple* (1675) by Thomas Comber is designed to assist in 'the daily use' of the Prayer Book. Its preface has as its central theme that of proving 'the reasonableness of our being present at daily Prayers, to those who say they cannot'. Nelson's preface makes a plea to his fellow-laymen for a disciplined obedience to the Church's Way in daily life in order that 'we are blessed with what good men wish for, and bad men fear'. He praises the members of the religious societies of the day in this regard, for 'their regular conformity and obedience to the laws of the Church', their sacramental piety and their practical charity. We recall how Boyle and Bonnell supported and approved the religious practice of these societies. The Preface also recommends the use by the laity of spiritual directors and it suggests that 'if ever a Convocation should think fit to revise the catechism of the Church' questions should be added dealing with the nature and authority of the Sacred Ministry.

Nelson seems to have had great personal charm and was a life-long friend of Tillotson who died in his arms in 1694. As a young man he went to Paris with his friend from schooldays, the astronomer Edmund Halley through whose efforts Newton's *Principia* saw the light. Like most wealthy young men of the time Nelson made the grand tour. His was a mixed marriage, to Lady Theophila Lucy, a widow, but the lack of a shared allegiance did not mar their affection. He had Jacobite leanings and spent a good deal of time on the Continent and on his return to England he joined the Nonjurors, becoming intimate with all their leading figures. However, when William Lloyd, last but one of the deprived bishops died, both Nelson and Dodwell left the Nonjurors, the surviving bishop Thomas Ken having said to Nelson that the schism should be healed. Robert thus came back to the Church which spiritually he had never left, receiving the sacrament on Easter Day 1710 from his friend Archbishop Sharp of York. He was active in the affairs of the SPCK and the SPG and in many charitable undertakings. He wrote a *Life* of his former tutor Bishop George Bull whose *Defence of the Nicene Faith* (1685) was widely acclaimed by theologians at home and abroad, but it is his *Companion* with its simple question and answer format which did so much to educate the Anglican laity after Nelson's death in 1715. He could not think 'how better to employ that leisure and command of time which the good providence of God has entrusted me with, than by consecrating it to this service'. He affirms it to be a fitting task 'for a layman . . . when so many in the same rank' attack religion. His modesty obliges him to speak of 'the meanness of this performance', his only object being that of serving the practice of real religion. The reader is asked to pray 'for the unworthy author . . . that while he is sollicitous about the salvation of others, he may not fall short in securing his own'. Surely, in this period, the phrase 'the people of God' takes on a newly vivid meaning in the life and work of so many of the *laos*.

Some Others

'And what shall I more say? For the time would fail me to tell' of the spiritual pilgrimage of all those whose story is known to us, compassed about as they were with so great a cloud of unknown witnesses, fellow-members of the household of faith, all 'looking to Jesus, the author and perfector of our faith'. The reality and the truth of the Church is perceived in every generation in and through the lives of those in whom by means of the Word and Sacraments the Life of Christ Risen continues, influencing those with whom they have to do: 'Let your whole life be a line of direction to yourselves and of instruction to others'. So wrote Sir Henry Slingsby in *A Father's Legacy to His Sons* which he put on paper just before his execution as a royalist in 1658. The *Legacy* describes what a Christian household should be like and contains those words so indicative of the kind of religion for laypeople which we have been studying in lives, not in books: 'Make devotion your constant Diary to direct you'.[35]

In fact, such households were the nurseries of Anglican piety and A. Tindal Hart has illustrated this in his account of Squire Bruen of Bruen Stapelford in Cheshire. A puritan royalist favouring episcopacy and devoted to the Prayer Book, his own life of religious discipline and his abounding charity to the poor made his home such a centre for real religion that neighbouring gentry put their children to board at his house. He himself rose in the small hours for private devotions and meditation before assembling the household for prayers. On Sundays with all his family and servants 'leaving neither cook nor butler behinde him' and collecting tenants and neighbours *en route* he headed for Tarvin church – 'so was his godly example a great encouragement to others'.[36] Like Walton, he was a keen angler, and, unusually for those days, he never took strong drink though permitting it to be served at his table for others. Horton Davies has described the Bruen household as 'a vignette of Anglican piety'.

At the centre of such households, though not always noticeably so at first sight, was a wife and mother. What student of the period cannot but be moved by Jeremy Taylor's superb funeral sermon for the young Countess of Carbery, dead in childbirth and to whom he had ministered as pastor and friend both in health and sickness? He himself called his tribute 'a drawing in water colours' and it is indeed a gentle picture of a beautiful Christian life, not a conventional panegyric. Sensitively and with great delicacy Taylor depicts her passing: 'She was tender to pain, and apprehensive of it . . . but God that knew her fears . . . fitted her with a death so easy, so harmless, so painless, that it did not put her patience to a severe trial'. Though nobly born, he tells us, her humility desired that she should be known only for herself and only 'esteemed honourable according to that which is the honour of a Christian'. An heiress and exposed to all the temptations of society, she was chaste and 'not capable of uncivil temptation'. She practised her religion with modesty and devotion, her husband encouraging her 'with good books'. Daily she read her Bible 'to instruct her in the knowledge and love of God and of her neighbours'. She was 'constant at her prayers', at reading and meditating. Her religion, says Taylor, was the genuine article: 'it took root downward in humility, and brought forth fruit upward in the substantial graces of a Christian'. 'She was also a constant reader of sermons' and her last plan, defeated by death, was the compiling of a large book 'in which she purposed to have a stock of religion transcribed in such assistances as she would choose, that she might be readily furnished and instructed to every good work'.

As one considers this 'drawing in water-colours' what emerges is not an aristocratic religious blue-stocking, but a charming young matron, bringing up her large family, managing a great household, charitable to the poor and generous and encouraging to her servants, 'hugely loving to oblige others', intelligent and well-read. The practice of her religion, says Taylor, made her what she was, for 'it dwelt upon her spirit, and was incorporated with the periodical work of every day'.[37]

Another such was Mrs Margaret Godolphin, who died at the age of twenty-six in giving birth to her first baby. When she took ill her husband sent post haste for John Evelyn with whom she had a deep spiritual affinity and who advised them both in 'secular concernes'. She had 'received the heavenly *Viaticum* but the Sunday before' and 'the king himselfe and all the Court expressed their sorrow, and to the poore and most miserable it was irreparable'. Her custom was to visit the sick and afflicted and she dispensed 'great charities all her lifetime' using Evelyn as her almoner. 'She was most deare to my Wife, affectionate to my children, interested in my concernes, in a word, we were but one soule'. Her death was a great grief to Evelyn who called her 'my blessed Saint, lovely in death'. He had to make all the funeral arrangements, Margaret's husband being physically prostrated by shock. Later, he and Evelyn together went through her papers and found them to be chiefly prayers, meditations and compositions of her own 'as if she had been all her life a student of Divinity'. John Evelyn wrote a life of her 'for what she read, or writt, she liv'd'. Here once again is this deep-down religious practice which has the attractiveness for others which genuine religion seems always able to exercise. When Evelyn's beloved daughter Mary died of the small-pox, aged nineteen, her heartbroken father recalled with sorrow and gratitude her beauty, intelligence and piety: 'I never saw, or knew her equal . . . save in one onely Creature of her Sex, Mrs Godolphin, (late the Wife of my Lord Godolphin) whose life for the singular piety, vertue and discretion. (and that she was to me a friend, in all the peculiar transcendencys of that relation) I have written at large . . . and this I mention here, because the example of that most religious lady: made I am assured deepe impressions on my deare child; and that I was told she caused it to be read to her, at the very beginning of her sicknesse'.[39] Mary was beautiful, sought in marriage by 'no lesse than foure gent: of quality'. 'She sang and daunc'd with the most grace that in my whole life I had ever seene'. It was intended to offer her the post of Maid of Honour to the Queen but she was put off by the immorality of Court circles. She treated the servants with respect and affection, reading to them and praying with them if they were sick as did James Bonnell. Evelyn gave her the run of his study and she read history and the classics, 'all the best romances and modern poems, and could compose very happily'.

All these young women belonged to the upper reaches of English society. They were rich, intelligent and attractive and they took the practice of their religion very seriously indeed. This is what Anglican religious practice at its best looked like in the seventeenth century. The devotional programme of the extended families of the Ferrars at Little Gidding and of Susanna Hopton at Credenhill serves to concentrate the picture and to highlight the spirituality which motivated and informed the religious ideals and practice of the period. The poet-mystic, Thomas Traherne, whose devotion was shaped by the Prayer Book, was a member of Mrs Hopton's group and later he wrote for her his *Centuries of Meditations*. The Ferrar group, of about thirty persons, became famous in their own day and received such different visitors as the King and the carping author of *The Arminian Nunnery*. Walton in his *Life* of Herbert describes their regime which revolved around the Daily Offices and the reading of the whole Psalter at fixed hours in one day: 'And this course of piety and great liberality to his poor neighbours, Mr Farrer maintained till his death, which was in the year 1639'.

4
Anglican Spirituality – the liturgical and moral-ascetical components

'This is the famous stone
That turneth all to gold;
For that which God doth touch and own
Cannot for lesse be told'.
                    – George Herbert

IT is all very well as far as it goes to hold up as examples of the spirit of Anglicanism in practice the lives of those men and women which we have been examining. But for our own sakes as well as for the better understanding of their religious practice we need to go deeper. *What sort of ideal were they striving through grace to realize, and what sort of pattern was being set before them?* What is the nature of Anglican spirituality? Spirituality is a nuanced word and one which is often used and understood today in a vague, fuzzy way. Precision is needed here if we are to come within reach of our objective. The dictionary points us in the right direction with its tertiary definition of spirituality as 'a distinctive approach to religion or prayer'. So then we are trying to discover what characteristics or qualities are native and integral to the Anglican understanding of devotion and of religious practice. Martin Thornton helps to fill this out for us: 'Spirituality is not isolated pietism; it is concerned with prayer, worship, and Christian discipline, which colour and inspire the whole of life. Furthermore, personal devotion and private life are indissociable from liturgy and theology'.[1] Now we feel we are getting somewhere and all of a sudden aspects of those lives we have been looking at are thrown into high relief. James Bonnell's meditations, his twice daily churchgoing and sacramental devotion, his discipline, his personal integrity and his abundant charity,

52

his deliberate attempt to grow in the virtues, all suddenly fall into place. Thornton's picture of spirituality suddenly comes to life, and we are reminded of William J. Wolf's definition of spirituality: 'practice that makes religion come to life. Spirituality is 'piety' or 'devotion' that infuses the whole of life with prayer, worship and discipline'.[2] Is there then a pattern here, having distinctive features and designs, which is the most typical representation, the quintessence, of Anglican spirituality?

It appears to me that the weave of Anglican piety has in and through it two closely intertwining components which together create a definite design. These are the liturgical component and the component of moral/ascetical theology. Interacting upon each other and at times fusing into a single instrument they produce a spirituality which has marked characteristics.

The Liturgical Component

It is common coin nowadays amongst students of our heritage to underline, as does Daniel B. Stevick, that 'Any account of Anglican spirituality must give the Book of Common Prayer a primary place'.[3] David Siegenthaler puts it even more strongly: 'The Book of Common Prayer is informative for Anglicans not only for definition of doctrine and polity but as well for the content and style of spirituality. *That book is the matrix*. The concerns and consequences of corporate worship are the concerns and consequences of personal worship. In its simplest terms this means that Anglican spirituality is personal but never private, never detached from an individual's engagement with the community and with the world'.[4] That comment is illuminating as we attempt to uncover the pattern of Anglican spirituality which, says Urban T. Holmes, 'grows out of liturgical prayer, out of the sacraments rooted in the earth . . . Anglican piety emerges from a life steeped in *The Book of Common Prayer*.'[5] Does not the daily practice of those lives whose records we have been studying confirm this 'not in notion but in life' as Hamilton put it three centuries ago?

J. R. H. Moorman comments that 'many devout lay-people heard Mattins and Evensong every day in their parish church, or had the Offices said in their own homes, in the presence of the entire household'.[6] Moreover, one effect of the proscription of the Prayer Book under the Commonwealth was to drive it underground and cause it to be more highly valued and more dearly loved as a book of household devotion. At the Restoration, the Prayer Book came into the open again – Pepys records 'This day also did Mr Mills begin to read all the Common Prayer, which I was glad of'. The week before he notes that 'Mr Mills did begin to nibble at the Common Prayer'.[7] But underground and at illegally held services it had been at work during two decades producing a spirituality for daily living instead of what John Evelyn had complained of a few years previously 'that there was now nothing practical preached, or that pressed reformation of life, but high and speculative points and straines, that few understood'.[8]

As we stand back endeavouring to estimate or to quantify the influence of the Prayer Book on the religious practice of our forebears, it is not just that its mark can be traced in the poetry of Donne, Herbert and Traherne, or its liturgical excellences set out in the very many books on the Prayer Book which the century produced. What can hardly be overestimated is the impact on countless individuals and homes of the weekly or daily recitation of the Offices and of the liturgy in which a piety both domestic and communal, personal and corporate, was at work moulding hearts and minds. From 1678 onwards this was reinforced by the religious societies of young men 'who agreed to pray, if possible, seven times a day and keep close to the teaching of the Church of England by going daily to church and making their communion every Sunday and festival. In addition, they visited the poor, helped poor scholars at the universities, and engaged in other works of charity and mercy'.[9] We have noted how Boyle and Bonnell involved themselves with these societies. While Bonnell was alive to the danger of such groups becoming 'holy huddles' he saw the actual advantages as heavily outweighing this possible disadvantage.[10]

We find ourselves underlining William J. Wolf's comment that 'For Anglicans the Book of Common Prayer has itself been *the* devotional book . . . not just for clerics but for every member'.[11] When he continues that 'the actual impact of the Book of Common Prayer on Anglican spirituality often remains vague, unfocused and poorly articulated' we perceive that we have some spade-work to do.

As we sift the evidence from lives and contemporary writings which we have so far adduced, it would appear that the immediate point of impact of the Prayer Book on Anglican spirituality is quite simply in the constant recitation of the Offices creating consciously and unconsciously a distinctive approach to religion and prayer. As the *Eikon Basilike* (1648) put it, speaking of the Prayer Book, 'wholesome words, being known and fitted to men's understandings, are soonest received into their hearts, and aptest to excite and carry along with them judicious and fervent affections'.[12] It occurred to me to put this to the test in a personal way. Like all Irish Anglicans of my generation I was brought up exclusively on the 1662 Prayer book. From childhood its cadences were on my ear and its services were what I understood by the phrase 'going to church'. More important, as time passed the very wording of those services sank into my consciousness and became an expression of what I was beginning to understand religion to be all about. 'Steeped in the Book of Common Prayer' would be a factual description of those of my generation who were trying through grace and through failures to take our religion seriously. Accordingly, by way of experiment, I deliberately tried to exclude everything else from my mind and to encourage random passages from the Book of Common Prayer to echo in my thoughts. Quickly I discovered that the problem was to stop them echoing, for sentence after sentence chimed in my recollection: 'the devices and desires of our own hearts' (General Confession); 'a godly, righteous and sober life' (do.); 'grant us true repentance, and his Holy Spirit' (Absolution); 'envy, hatred and malice and all unchari-tableness' (Litany); 'hearty repentance and true faith' (Absolution); 'in love and charity with your neighbours'

(Invitation); 'these holy mysteries' (Post-Communion); 'that we may continue in that holy fellowship, and do all such good works as thou hast prepared for us to walk in' (Thanksgiving); 'an outward and visible sign of an inward and spiritual grace' (Catechism); 'the Body and Blood of Christ, which are verily and indeed taken and received by the faithful in the Lord's Supper' (Catechism); 'create and make in us new and contrite hearts' (Ash Wednesday Collect); 'serve and please thee in newness of life' (Confession).

At this point I caused the stream of consciousness to cease flowing though it showed no signs of doing so on its own. I can only guarantee that I wrote the sentences down as they came. There was no cheating through selective recollection! The point of the experiment is to ask what sort of spirituality is indicated by this chance collection of remembrances of worship over the years according to the Book of Common Prayer? Could it by any chance show us *in miniature* what was happening through time and place to countless men and women on the broader canvas of history as they strove to put their religion into practice?

What these unbidden and unselected remembrances suggest is a type of spirituality which a closer examination of the Prayer Book presents in further and clearer detail. It is a piety both liturgical and sacramental and a piety for wayfaring men. Faith and repentance are at its centre as is an awareness of the Holy Spirit's work in making us 'new creatures' in spite of the sins which do so easily beset us. There is about it a sense of being on pilgrimage and a pervading awareness of our responsibility for the living of our own lives in co-operation with the Spirit's grace. It is a living towards God in the service of the neighbour through Christ, who is both God and man, lawgiver and Redeemer. It is a spirituality deeply aware of mystery and at the same time a spirituality practicable by ordinary men and women. Prayer and meditation and affective devotion to Christ are there as is the following and imitation of Christ though the somewhat monastic, self-afflictive theme which sometimes surfaces in à Kempis is on the whole absent. Absent too are the piety of assurance and the predestinarian obsessions then current in some contemporary circles.

I believe that these are fair deductions which a more detailed perusal of the Prayer Book will convert into certainties. It is a spirituality which insists that Word and Sacrament are for living 'in newness of life', that worship is meant to send us out in the process of being remade, 'confirmed and strengthened in all goodness'. In a sentence, the Christian life is the recollected life and specifically seen as such by, for example, James Bonnell: 'I have nothing to do this half hour but to wait on my God', otherwise 'if we are in haste to do something else . . . it is a great hazard if ever we are recollected'. In other words, the moral/ascetical theology component so strongly affirmed in the Anglican tradition is there also all the time in the Prayer Book, merging with and becoming part of the purely liturgical component. We recall Thornton's definition and we realize that here it is being given substance and actuality: 'Spirituality is not isolated pietism; it is concerned with prayer, worship, and Christian discipline which colour the whole of life'. Before we pass on to discover how this other component develops in the practice and in the devotional manuals of the period, we ought to look briefly at two matters. These are the structures of the Book of Common Prayer and the role of the *Companion* books which did so much to spread and to deepen the liturgical element in Anglican spirituality.

To consider the Prayer Book's structure is not to embark on a lengthy dissection of the form and content of its services. Rather is it simply to note that it has a basic structure and that this has its bearing on spirituality as understood and practised by Anglicans. Thornton has pointed out that the Prayer Book's structure is that of the *Regulum* of St Benedict. This is the threefold rule of prayer, the common office (*opus Dei*) supporting private prayer (*orationes peculiares*) both of which are allied to, and consummated by, the eucharist: 'this forms the over-all structure of the Book of Common Prayer'. Most significantly for our thesis, he goes on to affirm that 'the threefold Rule of prayer is absolutely fundamental to all

Catholic spirituality'.[13] This is the pattern which Caroline commentators on the Prayer Book saw in the Anglican liturgy and its influence on Caroline spirituality can be seen in many of the devotional manuals of the period. 'Anglican spirituality is Prayer Book spirituality' writes Harvey H. Guthrie in the sense that 'the ascetical *genre* of the Book of Common Prayer is that of the *Regulum* which makes it possible for the basis of the spiritual life of a community of Christian people to be the corporate, liturgical, sacramental and domestic life of that community itself'.[14]

I would submit that the evidence for this is in the lives which we have been studying. How this structure has been clothed in a specific spirituality is already indicated in the text of the liturgy itself and in the practice of those who used it. This is revealed in detail and in depth when we come to assess the moral/ascetical component and the devotional works in which the century abounded.

That 'the Prayer Book conceives of each service in the liturgy as the work of the whole body of the faithful'[15] is something amply documented in all Anglican liturgical writings and in the efforts made to increase participation by seeing and hearing what was being done in church. Liturgists like Cosin, Anthony Sparrow and Hamon L'Estrange sought to expound the *rationale* of Anglican worship in their books.[16] These achieved a wide circulation but it was the companion type which did most to encourage devotion, books like Thomas Comber's *A Companion to the Temple*, William Nicholl's *A Comment on the Book of Common Prayer* and the most successful of them all, the layman Robert Nelson's *Companion to the Festivals and Fasts of the Church of England*. Of this latter Dr Johnson claimed that no book save the Bible had greater sales. Nelson wrote that 'I have long thought a design of this nature might be serviceable to the interest of religion, and might contribute something towards reviving the piety and devotion of the Primitive times; to which I wish we were as conformable in our practices, as I am well satisfied we are in our doctrines'.[17] He praises the religious societies for the constant and devout attendance of their members at the

Prayer Book services and notes how this promotes a piety and practical charity, reviving 'that true spirit of Christianity, which was so much the glory of the Primitive times'.[18] In the same way, Comber's *Preface*, urging 'the reasonableness of the daily attendance on publique Prayers' comments that 'so did the primitive Christians'. He puts his finger on the basic point we have been stressing, namely, the influence of the liturgy on spirituality: 'And truly it is to be doubted that constant neglecters of publique Prayers, use seldom and slight devotions in private'. He affirms that liturgical worship is 'a rich treasury of all that can make our devotion lively and useful'. It is his hope that his commentary on the Prayer Book will 'suggest a way to all devout souls for making pathetical and pious enlargements, more and better than are to be found here; that so our daily Offices may be full of life and pleasure'. Comber is saying in effect that *praying the liturgy produces prayer, that the Prayer Book creates spirituality for men just as men have created the Prayer Book.*

This last point that the Book of Common Prayer is a human compilation of its age and setting leads to a brief but relevant digression, namely, *why then revise it?* Perhaps the short answer is that we are doing with it exactly what our ancestors did at several specific times. The point is well taken in the American symposium from which I have quoted. Stevick writes: 'But the work which took its shape in the sixteenth century has often been gratefully and creatively *repossessed*. The original drafters of the English Prayer Book did not set out to produce a devotional and liturgical classic or a monument of English prose. Their task was quite functional: to issue, in a rather short time for so large an undertaking, a serviceable, vernacular liturgical text for use throughout the reformed Church of England'. He reminds us that 'this generation knows, as few since 1549 could have, that the Prayer Book is made by the Church. The great catholic liturgical heritage has been *repossessed and refashioned* by a Church freshly taking responsibility for its own life of worship and prayer. Unmistakably, we make the Prayer Book. Yet in a profounder sense, the Prayer Book makes us. *We are not so much its parents as its grateful children.* The very lessons in faith which inform our impulse to change it have been taught by it. It has its own vitality and its own integrity . . . the Prayer Book can only be revised responsibly by those who have first respected it, listened to it and been *nurtured* by it'.[19] That is well and truly said and I believe that, by and large, liturgical revision has heeded the warning given thirty years ago by Martin Thornton. Agreeing that updating and adapting to modern need is necessary now as it was in the past, he advised that 'All that is work for the living Church, for the worshipping community being boldly experimental under the guidance of sane authority. Let us, guided by the liturgical experts, proceed with the job – new Offices, revised eucharistic liturgy, new rites for occasional services. But for goodness' sake *let us leave the basic structure alone*'.[20]

Like the authors of that symposium I now worship mainly through the medium of the Revised or Alternative Prayer Book, but the Prayer Book of 1662 can never be forgotten or ignored. Twentieth-century Anglicans must repossess it in the idiom of their times that it may be as creative for modern spirituality as it was for that of our forebears in the household of faith. It is not irrelevant to recall that even at the end of the seventeenth century Comber found it necessary to explain to the worshipper such phrases from the Litany as 'in all time of our wealth' and 'sudden death'. Of the first, he notes 'that is, in the old dialect and original signification of the word, of our welfare and prosperity' and 'sudden death' he points out, means 'untimely death'.[21] Language is constantly and imperceptibly changing, now enriching itself, now impoverishing itself. Nelson reminds us that matters liturgical and changes in worship are rightly part of the due authority of the Church: 'Except we will acknowledge some power in the Church, to determine the modes and circumstances of public worship, and to oblige us in indifferent matters, it is impossible there should be any settled frame of things in any Christian Society in the world'.[22] The spirituality which is formed by liturgical worship, says Nelson, is that of duty to God, our neighbour and ourselves.[23] Comber echoes him in his comment on 'a godly, righteous and sober life' in 'the daily Confession'. We are called 'to live hereafter in piety to God, charity with others, temperance towards ourselves'.[24] The same threefold pattern (deriving from 'soberly, righteously and godly' in Titus 2. 11–13) forms the whole structure of one of the most enduring devotional manuals of the day, Jeremy Taylor's *The Rule and Exercises of Holy Living* (1650): 'Christian religion . . . according to the apostle's arithmetic, hath but these three parts of it; 1. Sobriety, 2. Justice, 3. Religion'.[25] This then would seem to be the point at which we turn to see how this spirituality is enlarged upon and developed in detail by considering the form and content of a selection of the devotional writings used, like John Cosin's *Collection of Private Devotions* (1637), as 'an integral and homogeneous *private* complement to the *Common* Prayer of the Church'.

The Moral/Ascetical Theology Component and the Books of Devotion

It is no accident that seventeenth-century Anglicans called moral theology 'practical divinity'. Moreover, they so reformed that science that moral and ascetical theology were fused in one instrument, its subject being not so much the penitent-at-the-tribunal as the Christian-in-the-Church. In this, the Anglicans anticipated the major developments of the twentieth century producing the integrated science of moral-ascetical theology, the art of full co-operation with grace, in a total Christian life. The effect of this on the spirituality of the period was far-reaching and deserves some analysis and assessment.

As a lead-in, I would venture to characterize Anglican spirituality of the Caroline age as a spirituality of the four D's: *devotion, duty, discipline and detail*. A fifth D, doctrine, is always an ingredient in the mix. How this 'practical divinity' worked out in close harness with liturgical devotion to create a distinctive spirituality must now claim our attention.[26] The trend-setters here were the moral theologians Robert Sanderson and Jeremy Taylor. By fusing moral and ascetic theology into one science for Christian living they made the subject supremely practical for the spirituality of all who live through a Life not their own, transmitted to them by the Spirit through the means of grace, the Book and the Bread, within the eucharistic fellowship of the baptized who share in the apostolic faith. Sanderson's definition is seminal: 'But when all is done, positive and practique Divinity is it must bring us to Heaven: that is, it must poise our judgements, settle our consciences, direct our lives, mortify our corruptions, increase our graces, strengthen our comforts, save our souls . . . There is no study to this, none so well worth the labour as this, none that can bring so much profit to others, nor therefore so much glory to God, nor therefore so much comfort to our own hearts as this'.[27] Taylor succintly describes moral-ascetic theology as 'the life of Christianity' and 'the life of religion'.[28] The picture that emerges as we study the Anglican writers of the period is really one of the meaning of membership, of responsible discipleship, of growth in grace, of incorporation in Christ, 'if any man be in Christ he is a new creature'. In fact *kainē ktisis*, the new creation, is written large over the whole picture of Anglican spirituality.

Nobody seems to have noticed how these theologians anticipated most if not all the features of the quiet revolution in modern moral theology which has changed it from a largely juristic science into a science of response and responsibility in discipleship. In our day, the changes began with Gilleman's *Primacy of Charity in Moral Theology* (1959) which complained that the current manuals were on the wrong tack because they 'do not formulate morality with sufficient reference to the interior life, which is left to a special branch of theology called spirituality', precisely the point made by the Caroline writers. In the same year his fellow Roman Catholic, Bernard Häring, in *The Law of Christ* came nearer still: 'We understand moral theology as the doctrine of the imitation of Christ . . . The point of departure in Catholic moral theology is Christ, who bestows on man a participation in His life and calls on him to follow the Master'. He further defines the subject as 'a moral theology where primary concern should be to restate the perfect ideal of the whole Christian life and to underline the means of attaining it'. Josef Fuchs sees moral theology as 'an unfolding . . . of Christ's call to us, of the vocation of believers in Christ'.[29] A modern Anglican, Herbert Waddams puts it with simplicity: 'It can hardly be stated too strongly that moral theology is basically dealing with our life as it is lived in union with Christ'.[30] In short, what we all now take for granted was in fact the complete reform of the moral/ ascetical component which was formative for spirituality and which was first brought about by the Anglican moral theologians whose primary concern was with the re-creation through grace of the human person. Their avowed aim, as set out by such as Beveridge, Taylor and William Nicholson, was to make man 'a new creature' 'sincere in his obedience', a favourite phrase which throws further light on what they meant by 'the perfection of wayfaring men'. This was the ideal which was being presented to the members of the Church. It is clearly brought out by, for example, William Nicholson in his *Plain and Full Exposition of the Catechism* (1655). Talking about 'the perfection of wayfaring men', for absolution perfection is not expected from us in this life, he reminds us that to attain such a state grace is needed. Even then grace does not bring about in man 'an unsinning obedience, but it makes him 'a new creature', creates in him a sincere obedience to the whole Gospel'. This concept of a wayfarer's perfection (*perfectio viatorum*) involves response to grace and responsibility in obedience. Jeremy Taylor stressed this: 'The state of regeneration is perfection all the way, *even when it is imperfect in its degrees* . . . sincerity is the formality or the soul of it; and the mercies of God accepting it in Christ, and assisting and promoting it by his Spirit of grace, is the third part of its constitution, it is the spirit'.[31] Bernard Häring spoke for modern moral theology: 'There is no surer way to the full perfection of the whole man than the perfect following of Christ in the communal life of the Church'.[32]

A new kind of moral/ascetical theology was visualised by the Carolines through the merging into one of what had long been seen and handled as two distinct instruments. The

Anglicans saw themselves as re-siting moral theology within the *kerygma*, the totality of the Gospel. Consequently, theirs is a moral theology of the new law, the new life and the new creature and this appears constantly in the seventeenth-century writings. Inevitably therefore and as part of this emphasis they determined to replace *penitentia* by *metanoia*, the New Testament concept of repentance. This they saw as a deliberate element in the re-structuring of a moral theology of the Kingdom. Leaving aside as not specially relevant to our theme here the technical analysis by the Caroline theologians of repentance, of contrition and attrition, it is sufficient to stress that their discussion of repentance has all to do with a new quality of life in Christ. Thus, Taylor calls repentance 'a whole state of the new life, an entire change of the sinner'.[33] Payne agrees: 'Repentance is the same thing in Scripture with Conversion, Regeneration, the New birth, the New Creature, the New Man, and the like'.[34] William Wake at the turn of the century understood repentance as 'a real conversion . . . a change of life'.[35] Deliberately I have refrained from going into the careful detail in which the Anglican writers evaluated all the aspects of the question. I have done so because it is enough for our picture of the kind of spirituality which they were endeavouring to create to underline the vital importance they attached to fostering in each individual what Sanderson called 'a conscience made of obedience'. *This is at the heart of Caroline spirituality*. The personal responsibility of the individual in moral action must be guided by his own reason. Archbishop Sharp wrote 'We do believe that in matters where a man's conscience is concerned, everyone is to be a judge for himself, and must account for himself'. This is typical as is Sharp's further comment that this does not preclude a man from seeking spiritual counsel and absolution in particular cases, as the Book of Common Prayer advises.[36] With one voice, the moral/ascetical theologians of seventeenth-century Anglicanism echo Taylor's 'the Gospel is nothing else but faith and repentance' and Payne's 'repentance is the whole practical condition of Christianity, and together with faith, makes up the entire duty of the Christian'. Despite a range of emphasis in defining repentance, contrition and attrition,[37] the Prayer Book's indispensable linkage between faith and repentance (as in the Holy Communion invitation, the Catechism and the Homilies) is seen as essential to the spirituality held up as a realisable ideal to the members of Christ's Family. Finally, and closely linked to a restating of the Scriptural concept of repentance is a distinct Caroline unease about the distinction between mortal and venial sin as they then understood its meaning and application. Sharp wrote 'Their distinction of sins into two sorts, mortal and venial, is sufficiently known – Which distinction *as they order it*, is really an hindrance to repentance; or breeds in every man, that embraceth that distinction, such a false notion of repentance, that he cannot in reason think himself obliged to set himself upon the mortifying and the forsaking several habits of sin which he may find himself guilty of'.[38] Taylor makes the same point that just as moral theology needs to be clear as to the meaning of repentance so the latter concept requires to understand what the distinction implies. It is not that the Anglicans thought all sins to be equal. On the contrary, they distinguished sins of ignorance, infirmity and presumption, sins of weakness and of wilfulness, sins of malice and infirmity. Their objection to the current distinction was to the idea that any sin by its nature had an inherent right to pardon because this helped to lower Christian standards. Moreover, by establishing such a classification of sins moral theology was effectively returned to being a juristic science rather than an instrument for promoting holiness of life. Taylor said 'To distinguish a whole kind of sins is a certain way to make repentance and amendment of life imperfect and false'. The dangers are, in his view, that a false kind of spirituality of the calculator and of the second-best is promoted: 'It is rather a dispensation or leave to commit one sort of them' and 'Men call what they please venial'.[39] Aware of the subtle complexity of being human he observes that 'no sin is absolutely venial but in comparison with others: neither is any sin at all times and to all persons alike venial'. Similarly, 'If any man about to do an action of sin, enquires whether it be a venial sin or no, – to that man, at that time, that sin cannot be venial'.[40]

Without exception, the Caroline writers on the spiritual life take up this subject and deal with it, often at length.[41] What concerns us here is not so much the details of their analysis as their reason for treating the matter as important. In a sentence, it is because the spirituality they strove to inculcate is a spirituality of discipleship rather than one of spiritual book-keeping. All the time, it is a question of standards, of serious commitment, for those who are alive to their imperfections as they try through grace to follow the Saviour and so seek a spirituality which, as John Hales put it, 'does mix itself with every part of our life'.[42] If at times we think that we can detect in some of the writers an air of too much austerity this is in part due to an over-reaction on their part against what seemed to them to be laxity.

How they were helped towards the realizing of the ideal will be seen in some of the devotional books of the century.

5

Anglican Spirituality – a distinctive character

'All books of devotion he read with a very sensible pleasure'
– Hamilton on Bonnell

YEARS ago I came upon what I can only describe as a whole chorus of Synges. There were five of them, all bishops of the Church of Ireland in the seventeenth and early eighteenth centuries and all closely related. The best known is Edward Synge, Archbishop of Tuam, born in 1659 in Inishannon, Co. Cork where his father, later to be Bishop of Cork, was rector. It was said of Edward that his position in ecclesiastical biography is unique: the son of one bishop and the nephew of another, himself an archbishop and the father of two bishops. His *Essay on Catholic Christianity* was well-known in his day and was regarded as the best answer 'to the plain man seeking a system on which to order his life'.[1] Of the archbishop it was recorded that what he wrote he believed, and what he believed he practised. His contemporaries valued him as a devotional writer. Two of his books, his *Plain and Easy Method* and his *Essay toward making the Knowledge of Religion Easy* are examples of the kind of spirituality shared with those English colleagues whose works we have been considering. Synge's is the same strong, practical piety of faith and repentance, of obedience and of three-fold duty to God, man and ourselves. His uncle George, bishop of Cloyne, was also a writer and they were all ancestors of John Millington Synge whose play, *The Playboy of the Western World*, one of the great plays of world literature, occasioned a riot in the Abbey Theatre, Dublin, on its opening night in January 1907. I refer to Synge mainly to show that geography and nationality made no difference to the kind of religion and the type of spirituality nourished and fostered by Anglicanism in the seventeenth century. Bonnell in Dublin and Nelson in Paris and Evelyn in London all saw the same ideal and all strove to realize it for themselves in the same way and by the same means. It was, I have suggested, a spirituality composed of four separable strands which were in practice closely interwoven – *devotion, duty, discipline and detail.* If we examine a selection of the devotional books of the period under these headings artificially separated but which in reality are nevertheless interdependent components of a total and unified spirituality, we shall be able, I believe, to hear what A. M. Allchin has called 'voices speaking to us from our own past with words we should be able to hear today'.[2] He is writing about Anglican spirituality past and present: 'Throughout the centuries there has been the practice both of the inner life of prayer and meditation, and of the outward life of liturgy and service in the world, which has been reflected in manuals of devotion, commentaries on Scripture and the Prayer Book, collections of sermons and meditations, works of poetry and prose alike'. He goes on to draw our attention today to 'the fact that Anglicans are heirs to a tradition of which at the present they are often almost unaware. There is here a need for a recovery of memory, which will allow for a recovery of identity'.

There in a couple of sentences is the objective of this book.

As to the extensive devotional material used by our forebears my own evaluation would be that the books fall into three more or less distinct categories but with some natural and inevitable overlap. There are the purely devotional manuals and there are the books in which practical direction is combined with devotion and there are the catechetical books. This third type concerns itself with what might be termed the end-product of moral/ascetical theology, namely the attitude to religion and life which this spirituality strove to create in the members of the Church. Let us see if we can form some sort of picture of how all these handbooks combined with the Prayer Book to produce a distinctive approach to religion and prayer, a spirituality characteristic of Anglicanism. We shall attempt to do this by way of examining what I conceive to be its four main components.

I
The Four D's

Under these headings we look first at some of the purely devotional manuals. These are the rarest class but even in them the totality of the Christian's calling in the world makes itself felt. Among the earliest of these is *The Devotions* of Lancelot Andrewes first published in English in 1630. The *Preces Privatae* was originally written in Greek and Latin and there was an Oxford edition in 1675 and an earlier one in 1648. Andrewes is said to have been skilled in fifteen languages and his book of prayers was for his own use and never meant for publication. In spite of this, it has become part of the treasury of Anglicanism, carrying, as Dean Church said, the spirit of the Prayer Book 'from the Church to the closet'.[3]

What can we learn about the pattern of Anglican devotion from this bishop who helped to prepare the Authorized Version of the Bible in 1611, who was constantly about the Court as a member of the Privy Council yet displayed a concerned and wide charity embracing the poor, the sick and criminals? What sort of piety do we discern in this theologian who answered Bellarmine but who according to contemporaries, Buckeridge and Isaacson, spent 'a great part of five hours every day . . . in prayer and devotion to God'?[4] That the book is the private prayer book of a scholar is clear from the use of so many of the Fathers and of early and later liturgies unobtrusively woven with the words of Scripture into morning and evening prayers, meditations, confession and intercession. Yet because of its beauty and absence of self-preoccupation generations after him have found that for them it expresses the mysteries of the Faith in relation to their daily lives and to the life of the society of which they are part. The prayers go deep into the experience of the individual's spiritual needs but the range of intercessions reminds him that he belongs to a Family. To each and every one he owes the duty of prayer and the exercise of the Seven Works of Mercy, and Christian Duty is the theme of one of the meditations. It is a beautiful book, the personal expression of a profound spirituality of the heart and of the mind. Many today, once they have accustomed themselves to its style, find in it a spirituality that is timeless.

Another such book of devotion is John Cosin's *Collection of Private Devotions* (1627).[5] Like the *Preces Privatae* there is little of the directional element and, as in Andrewes, the traditional element is stressed: the spiritual and corporal works of mercy, the seven root sins and the seven penitential psalms appear. Nevertheless, the moral/ascetical component is beginning to make itself felt in self-examination through the decalogue. Prynne wrote against it the year after it was published but it went into many editions. It is thought to have been written in the first place for Henrietta Maria's Court ladies and it was intended for use as a private complement to the Book of Common Prayer. It is in fact a very liturgical book, composed on the 'Hours' pattern, each Hour having its office with psalm, antiphon and lesson. There are devotional comments on the Church's Year and prayers are provided for all sorts of occasions. It provided a simple and practical pattern of devotion in a traditional style. Like Andrewes, Cosin gives intercessions and prayers of preparation for Holy Communion. It could have been entitled *The Way of the Church*.

When Archbishop Laud's *A Summarie of Devotions* was published posthumously in 1667, others were admitted to the private prayers of a Church leader and a theologian whose place in history none disputes though there are disputes about his policy, and whose death was reckoned by many as martyrdom for his Church: 'In that profession I have lived; and in that I come now to die'. The book 'written by his own hand' is arranged for the whole week with prayers for different hours of the day. As well as the Prayer Book collects, it has prayers from the Fathers, prayers for different occasions and for people of all classes. Similarly traditional in its devotional format is *The Practical Christian* (1673) by Richard Sherlock who lived an ascetic life in his wealthy parish and gave away most of his income to the poor. He too goes to the ancient liturgies for prayers but a change, heralded indeed by the book's title, is making itself felt. Direction for the spiritual life is becoming part of the devotional handbook. Sherlock calls his book 'a summary of Christian practice' and we see the internal and external aspects of spirituality merging as devotion and discipline, duty and detail combine to present a pattern of Christian behaviour. The Creed, baptismal promises and the decalogue are suggested for self-examination and his understanding of repentance is that of Caroline practical divinity. This mingling of the devotional and the directional soon became the most popular form.

The shift of emphasis can be seen in *Christian Consolations* (1671) thought to be by John Hacket who became bishop of Lichfield at the Restoration and attributed wrongly by Heber to Jeremy Taylor. It is designed as a 'manual of Christian consolations' derived from 'Five Helps and Directions for a Christian's Comfort', namely, faith, hope, the Holy Spirit, prayers and the Sacraments. As well as recommending traditionalist usage such as 'keeping canonical hours of prayer' and 'the night-offices of prayer, called vigils',[6] devotion to the Sacred Humanity in the Passion, ('a real union must follow between Christ and us'),[7] the element of discipline is noteworthy: 'Keep strictly as much as you are able' to times of prayer; 'Offer up not only your prayers, but the strict observation of set times'.[8] He insists that 'my Christian engagement . . . obligeth me to the strict discipline of my Lord . . . to *walk in newness of life*'.[9] Similarly, there is the attention to detail: 'prayer is the key to open the day, and the bolt to shut-in the night' but 'holy breathings, prayers like little posies, may be sent forth on every occasion'.[10] Perhaps the 'posies', like Robert Nelson's 'spiritual nosegay', are echoes of the *Devout Life* of S. Francis de Sales?[11] In any case, the classical Anglican book of devotion is emerging, and Bonnell's sacramental piety of devotion and discipline, of duty and detail, in the new life of incorporation and imitation, can be traced to its pattern in such books which he used to read 'with pleasure'.

While this is a sinewy spirituality for everyday use one notes that through it runs a richness of feeling, a strong vein of affective devotion. Out of the strength of Caroline spirituality comes forth sweetness. It is everywhere in the literature of the period, a piety of the heart as well as of the head and the hand. It recurs in Bonnell's sacramental meditations and is detailed and of imaginative realism 'with respect to every part of our Saviour's bitter Passion'.[12] It is in Taylor's *Great Exemplar* (1649) every bit as much as in his purely devotional manuals, for the book's central theme is the imitation of Christ: 'Every action of the life of Jesus, as it is imitable by us, is of so excellent merit, by making up the treasure of grace ... obtains of God grace to enable us to its imitation, by way of influence and impetration'.[13] Taylor's sturdy moral theologian's piety is warmed by a sensitive devotion to the Sacred Humanity, with a realism of detail like Bonnell's: 'he that comforts his brother in affliction, gives an amiable kiss of peace to Jesus ... we lead Jesus into the recesses of our heart by holy meditations, and we enter into his heart, when we express him in our actions'.[14] Taylor calls meditation going 'step by step with Jesus'. The same spirit fills Anthony Horneck's *The Crucified Jesus* (1686) and his Communion manual *The Fire of the Altar* (1683): 'Here is One that looks lovely in His blood, amiable in His wounds ... I that am poor and needy will wait to be refreshed by Thee'. William Beveridge fastens the communicant's gaze on the Sacred Humanity of the Crucified, dwelling on the physical details of the Passion, 'and all for our sins, even for ours'.[15] This is the pattern, seen in Robert Nelson's books and in *The Whole Duty of Man* (1658/9) – 'in the clefts of Thy Wounds shall be my refuge'.[16] We meet it, most beautifully expressed, in the almost equally popular *Practice of Divine Love* (1685) by Thomas Ken, bishop and hymn-writer. This richness of devotion always keeps its feet on the ground through being intimately linked with duty and discipline in a spirituality for which Jeremy Taylor's 'Live by rule' is an accepted imperative. *Affectivity is channelled through the discipline of meditation into the totality of the Christian life* in which the external and the internal elements of spirituality are formative of 'the new creature', of 'the walking in newness of life'. So Taylor insists that 'the use of meditation is, to consider any of the mysteries of religion with purposes to draw from it rules of life, or affections of virtue, or detestation of vice; and from thence a man rises to devotion, and mental prayer and intercourse with God; and, after that he rests himself in the bosom of beatitude, and is swallowed up with the comprehensions of love and contemplation. These are the several degrees of meditation'. He writes of the purgative way for beginners, the illuminative way for proficients and then, in the now familiar tone of that distinctive Anglican spirituality, he adds 'From hence if a pious soul passes to affections of greater sublimity . . . it is well; only remember . . . that still a good life is the effect of the sublimest meditation'. Beyond all this is the unitive way 'a prayer of quietness and silence . . . an immediate entry into an orb of light'.[17] One is reminded, if such reminder were necessary, that if this spirituality was designed for men and women trying to be Christian in the everyday world it was not a worldly spirituality, earth-bound and moralistic. We recall that little-known work of George Webb, bishop of Limerick, *The Practice of Quietness* (1633) with its subtitle 'Directing a Christian how to live quietly in this troublesome World': 'There is no practice next unto the practice of piety more excellent than the practice of quietnesse'. Not surprisingly much of what follows is simply moral/ascetical theology in action in the events and relationships of human life. Quietness and recollection are interior graces which have everything to do with being Christian in today's world.

What fascinates us about so many of these men is their indomitable loyalty and their ceaseless industry in the Church's cause in wretched circumstances. It tells us almost as much about the quality of their spirituality and about the meaning of responsible membership as do their writings. Taylor, three times imprisoned and driven from his parish; Hammond, deprived and imprisoned and then forced into retirement; Bramhall, a penurious exile with a price on his head; Hall, ejected from his bishopric of Norwich by the Puritans – and yet from each of them *the books kept coming*. Not just books in defence of the proscribed Church, but books of lasting spiritual and devotional value. Truly, the laity was well served.

The last-mentioned, Joseph Hall, was both a moral theologian and a devotional writer and as his work belongs to the first half of the century it provides a link with our second class of Anglican manuals in which the directional and the devotional are deliberately merged. Like Taylor he is a moral theologian and produced his *Resolutions and Decisions of Cases of Conscience* in 1649 a few years before the former issued his two major works on the subject. Like Taylor too he insists that meditation is not a luxury but a necessity and he has much to say about it in his numerous and popular devotional books such as *The Art of Divine Meditation*: 'this alone is the remedy of security and worldliness, and the pastime of saints, the ladder of heaven, and, in short, the best improvement of Christianity'.[18] He gives advice on how to prepare for and to persevere in meditation. Nothing can be achieved 'by snatches and uncertain fits'. He discusses methods of meditation and points out that a rule is a help, not an end in itself. Meditation 'begins in the understanding, endeth in the affection'.[19] It is clear from other books by Hall that he sees moral/ascetical theology as having one objective, the union of the Christian with Christ. This is the central theme of such works as *The Devout Soul* and *Holy Raptures*: 'Happy is the soul that is possessed by Christ'; 'Know that this union is not more mystical than certain'; 'it pleases God to unite the person of every believer to the person of the Son of God'. But for Hall this theology of mystical union has its firm base in a detailed religious practice of prayer and Bible-reading, of meditation and sacrament. For the graces of the Spirit we owe duties in return. Self-discipline is at the heart of devotion: 'This rigour is my peace'.[20] In his book *The Christian* we see the spirituality of a moral/ascetical theologian set out with all the Caroline insistence on detail, duty and discipline as essential to true devotion. Hall's output was remarkable and influential on his contemporaries. His advice, 'We feed on what we read, but we digest only what we meditate of'[21] was not for clerical consumption only. It penetrated elsewhere and the layman, Robert Nelson, gave the same counsel on meditation 'for it is by this method that we digest what we read'.[22]

II

I once asked a group of first-year clerical students if they could name any Anglican devotional writings of the Golden Age of Anglicanism. Hesitantly, and after a while, they came up with one book, Jeremy Taylor's *Holy Living*. It bears out Allchin's remark about Anglicans today being unaware of their heritage. We do indeed need a recovery of memory for the sake of our self-understanding because it is a rich inheritance.

The type of devotional book we are considering goes back a long way. In 1576 John Woolton published *The Christian Manuell, or of the life and manners of true Christians*. He was to become bishop of Exeter three years later and the theme of his book was to show 'how needefull it is for the servaunts of God to manifest and declare to the world: their faith by their deedes . . . and their profession by their conversation'. Indeed, to use an Irish expression, Woolton put his money where his mouth was by caring for the victims of the plague of 1570 in Exeter. We meet the emphasis, already becoming a hallmark of this spirituality, that 'all justified men should walk *in a new obedience*'[23] and he encourages daily self-examination with prayer as an essential devotional discipline. The suggestion will be recalled that a fifth D, doctrine, was never far beneath the surface in this spirituality. Constantly it is to be noticed in the general and explicit theological presuppositions of the writers and this is particularly the case in passages concerning the eucharist. We find the fifth D here in *The Christian Manuell* where teaching on justification by faith is sensibly related to doing good works and the test of faith is seen to be the good life.

A classic example of this piety of the five D's is a book which was said to be in the hands of everyone who could read, having been printed fifty times in English, apart from translations, by the year 1673. It is not certain when it was first published but the eleventh edition is dated 1619. The book is *The Practice of*

Piety which, one will recall, first led James Bonnell to 'the proposal of a methodical course of religion'.[24] It looks for sincerity of devotion instead of a formal religion, a devotion which affects the whole of our lives. There are prayers for all sorts of occasions, directions for Scripture-reading, for fasting and preparation for Holy Communion. It is a piety of detailed devotion and at the same time insists that the kernel of piety is to 'become a new creature', to be 'renewed by grace in Christ'. The author was Lewis Bayly who became Bishop of Bangor in 1616 and only one or two books amid the great number of such publications can have done as much to nurture Anglican spirituality in the seventeenth century. Bayly held that doctrine and practice are not separable and he began his manual with the doctrine of God believing that an understanding of His attributes was a necessary prerequisite for prayer and for a life of prayer and of the imitation of Christ. He writes too of the knowledge of man's self and the hindrances to 'the new life' among which he includes mistaking what justification by faith alone means, the point taken by Woolton. 'To be rich in good works, is the surest foundation of our assurance to obtain eternal life' writes Bayly and perhaps it comes as no surprise that John Bunyan read the book which his wife brought as part of her dowry.

It is borne in upon us that what was being held up as a pattern for Anglicans was no *à la carte* spirituality. It was deeply devotional and sane, disciplined and detailed, embracing the whole of a man's experience of living. It was demanding but rewarding. The concept of duty gave it muscle but it is duty understood within that love which is the fulfilling of the law. So Isaac Barrow could write 'Scripture . . . often expresses charity to be the fulfilling of God's law, as the best expression of all our duty toward God, of faith in Him, love and reverence of Him; and as either formally containing or naturally producing all our duty toward our neighbour'.[25] Here is the influence of the Prayer Book Catechism which everyone then learned by heart with its two Duties, each of which is a duty to love, to love God and the neighbour. They are followed in the Catechism by 'the Desire' insisting that these duties cannot be discharged without 'diligent prayer' and 'special grace'. This concept of duty is strong but not coldly self-reliant for it can only be performed through grace and in the spirit of devotion in the new life in Christ mediated by the Spirit through the Book and the Bread. The General Confession daily reminded worshippers of the threefold duty to God, the neighbour and one's self: 'a godly, righteous and sober life'.

'Concerning the particulars of this resolution of obedience, I need say no more, but that it must answer every part and branch of our duty'.[26] So runs *The Whole Duty of Man* in the section on preparing for Holy Communion. Here is a manual, probably the most influential of all, which became part and parcel of Anglican religious practice. Published in 1658 it continued as the standard book for the laity well on into the following century. Charles Simeon got a copy in 1779 'because it was the only religious book he had ever heard of, and read it with great diligence, fasting and crying to God for mercy'.[27] Eachard advised people to get it instead of books about 'experiences, getting Christ, and the like'.[28] It was to be found in most homes and in many churches. My own copy is an Irish printing published in Dublin 1727. Nobody knows who wrote it. It has been ascribed to John Fell, Richard Allestree, William Chappel, bishop of Cork, and to Henry Hammond who contributed a preface and clearly knew who the author was. During the Interregnum Hammond 'set himself' says R. S. Bosher 'to the task of building an intellectual defense for the faith whose outward structure lay in ruins'. Not only did he do this through his own numerous books but he encouraged others to write and the response was remarkable because the need was realized and acute. Bishop Duppa wrote 'Certainly there was never more need of the press, than when the pulpits are shut up'.[29] *The Whole Duty of Man* was part of the impressive output of Anglican writings during the decade between the execution of Charles I and the Restoration of his son.

The book begins with a preface 'Of the Necessity of Caring for the Soul', pointing out that the understanding, the will and the affections are 'disordered' and how can one hope for healing grace if this necessary duty is not undertaken? *The Whole Duty* is divided under seventeen Sundays followed by a selection of 'private devotions for several occasions' including prayers before and after 'receiving the blessed sacrament'. The prayers 'at the holy mysteries' reflect the same need for self-examination, repentance and grace, elaborated in Sunday 3 'Of the Lord's Supper' with its meditation 'when thou art at the Holy Table' on 'those bitter sufferings of Christ which are set out to us in the Sacrament'.

The themes of the Sundays cover our duties to God, of humility to His will, of honouring his Word and Sacraments, of worship and private prayer; our duties to ourselves, of sobriety, of avoiding pride, ambition and covetousness, of chastity and temperance; our duties to our neighbours, of justice, of eschewing covetousness, dishonesty and false behaviour, of peace-making and charity, of the dangers of envy. The special duties of parents and children, of marriage, of magistrates, pastors and employers are all examined. Clearly we can see here the combination of the two basic ingredients, the liturgical and the moral/ascetical elements. Sober and sacramental, it is never earth-bound but sees man's duty in the context of the love of God: 'There is a two-fold enjoying of God, the one imperfect in this life, the other more perfect and compleat in the life to come: that in this life is that conversation . . . which we have with God in his ordinances, in praying and meditating, in hearing his Word, in receiving the Sacraments, which are all intended for this purpose, to bring us into an intimacy and familiarity with God, by speaking to him and hearing him speak to us'.[30] A goal of practical duty is being set for the worshipper – the purpose of what is revealed in Scripture is to create a faith which issues in 'the bringing us to good lives'.[31] It is pattern piety of the period meant to supplement and accompany the Book of Common Prayer 'which for all publick addresses to God are so excellent and useful, that we may say of it, as David did of Goliath's sword, there is none like it'.[32] One might say that the dominant note of *The Whole Duty* is a spiritual matter-of-factness lending a fresh nuance to St Bernard's description of the Christian life as 'the business of all businesses'.

With the devotional writings of Jeremy Taylor a different note is struck though the composition is the same. *Holy Living* too is structured on our threefold duty but the almost pedestrian quality of *The Whole Duty* is replaced by the magic of style. Eminently practical as a moral/ascetical theologian Taylor is at the same time a poet writing in prose and one who is profoundly aware of the existence of mystery. His spirituality is at times mystical and always sacramental. The beatific vision is man's destiny through grace yet 'Live by rule' is his watchword and 'a strict course of piety'is part of *an integrated spirituality* in which devotion is compounded of strength and sweetness, of discipline and a rich affectivity.

Perhaps the ultimate assessment is that *seventeenth-century spirituality is holistic while that of our own times is an atomized spirituality*. When the expositor is one claimed subsequently as a literary genius something beautiful and unique is put at the disposal of those who long to grow in grace 'filling every corner of our heart with thoughts of the most amiable and beloved Jesus'.[33]

Holy Living then has basically the same framework as *The Whole Duty*: it is built around the threefold duty, 'soberly, righteously and godly'. This gives chapters on Christian sobriety, Christian justice and Christian religion. As in *The Whole Duty* the latter divides under faith, hope and love, and there is a valuable section on the external and internal acts of religion. The book closes with a wide range of prayers for almost every possible situation or eventuality. But it is in the way in which the framework is clothed that we see the difference. It is not simply that the style of writing carries one along and that the phrasing is often striking and that the prayers convey a warmth of devotion. There is more to *Holy Living* than this because it is rich with the perceptiveness, the knowledge and observation of the problems of being human, all seen and set out in the context of charity: 'Love is the greatest thing that God can give us; for Himself is love: and it is the greatest thing we can give to God; for it will also give ourselves, and carry with it all that is ours'.[34] Here too is wise and practical counsel on prayer, discerning passages on temperance, chastity, humility, modesty, envy and on repentance which 'of all things in the world, makes the greatest change'.[35] The section on 'preparation to the Holy Sacrament' has great theological and devotional depth, 're-presenting in this solemn prayer and sacrament, Christ as already offered' when the earthly table becomes a copy of the celestial altar: 'This is the sum of the greatest mystery of our religion; it is the copy of the passion, and the ministration of the great mystery of our redemption'.[36] Taylor, as well as the wide selection of occasional prayers, provides for 'ordinary days' a little lay-office for morning and evening, but sensibly advises the reader to take his pick according to his circumstances. He adds: 'Between this and noon, usually are said the daily mattins of the church, at which all the clergy are obliged to be present, and other devout persons, that have leisure to accompany them'. The plain reason for the superiority of *Holy Living* as compared with other equally popular manuals is the fact that its author is a skilled moral/ascetical theologian and spiritual counsellor who happens also to be a writer whose style is one of great distinction.

One has to resist the temptation to quote from *Holy Living* or from *Holy Dying* in the first chapter of which more perhaps than anywhere else he wrote prose as a poet. In conclusion, it is worth remembering another of his devotional books, *The Golden Grove* (1655), because it exemplifies the Caroline pattern of spirituality so simply. Incidentally, the book earned Taylor a spell of imprisonment in Chepstow Castle, his preface having suggested that Cromwell was 'the son of Zippor' *redivivus*. The section, *Agenda*, provides a religious diary for the day from rising to bedtime. 'Suppose every day to be a day of business', he writes, business that begins, continues and ends with prayer, at rising, at washing, at dressing. Then 'go to your usual devotions'. 'Before dinner and supper . . . let the public prayers of the church . . . be said publicly in the family'. There is counsel on meditation and on fasting. Prayers are provided for protection against each of the seven deadly sins. 'Make religion the business of your life' – truly it was no *à la carte* spirituality. Yet it is always preserved from fussiness by the ever-present recollection of the object and end of all the discipline and devotional detail – 'a new state of life', 'a changed course'. At the heart of spirituality for Taylor is the eucharist: 'These holy mysteries, being taken, cause that Christ shall be in us and we in Christ'.

Means and end are always before the reader of these manuals. Scougal's *The Life of God in the Soul of Man* (1677) sees the end as 'a real participation in the Divine Nature' and the means is discipline which opens our lives to faith and love, to humility and purity. The same theme is expounded by the Cambridge Platonist, Henry More, in his *Explanation of the Grand Mystery of Godliness* (1660): 'Obediential faith and affiance in the true God' issuing in charity, humility and purity, are the sources of this Life as it enters men's lives. Both writers unhesitatingly anchor the mystery of faith in regular devotion, meditation and Holy Communion. Let the layman Robert Nelson have the last word here. In *The Practice of True Devotion, in Relation to the End, as well as the Means of Religion* (1698) he asserts the end to be 'that we should become new creatures'. In truth *kainē ktisis* is writ large across Anglican spirituality. But the means, he adds, the 'exact performance of duties', while they are not ends in themselves are still indispensable: 'A man may be a bad man, and use them all; and yet there is no being good without them'.[37] That really says it all.

III
The Fifth D and
The Catechetical Books

In the Caroline pattern of instruction in the meaning of membership through preaching, catechism and personal spiritual counselling, a major element was catechesis. In his *Episcopal Charge* (1661) Jeremy Taylor enlarged on the importance of this threefold method: 'Let every minister teach his people the use, practice, methods and benefits of meditation or mental prayer . . . Let every minister exhort his people to a frequent confession of their sins, and a declaration of the state of their souls; to a conversation with their minister in spiritual things, to an enquiry concerning all parts of their duty: for by preaching and catechizing, and private intercourse, all the needs of souls can best be served; but by preaching alone they cannot'.

Anglicans saw catechesis as part of the Ministry of the Word and Hooker so understood and commended it: 'Catechizing may be in schools, it may be in private families. But when we make it a kind of preaching, we mean always the public performance in the open hearing of men'.[38] George Herbert in *The Country Parson* gives a whole chapter to the catechism 'to which all divinity may easily be reduced'. He writes 'The Country Parson values catechizing highly . . . He exacts of all the Doctrine of the Catechism; of the younger sort, the very words; of the older, the substance . . . He requires all to be present at Catechizing'. He perceived catechesis to be a doctrine-devotion synthesis: 'For there being three points of his duty; the one, to infuse a competent knowledge of salvation in every one of his flock; the other, to multiply and build up this knowledge to a spiritual temple; the third, to influence this knowledge, to press and drive it to practice, turning it to reformation of life, by pithy and lively exhortations; *Catechizing* is the first point, and but by Catechizing, the other cannot be attained'.[39]

Commenting on this catechism, preaching and guidance system, Martin Thornton says that its concern is with Christian living. But when he adds 'it is all ascetical theology, 'practical divinitie', spiritual direction', I think that like Herbert, we must qualify this since the fifth D, doctrine, is also at the centre of Caroline catechesis. So it was seen and understood by the authors of the various catechetical books who usually called them 'sums of divinity'. In view of the content of the Catechism it could hardly be otherwise and we have noted before that for the Caroline divines doctrine and devotion are not separable. They form a synthesis, a combination of both elements in a complex whole. The cumulative effect of the catechetical books on building up Anglicans in their faith when outwardly all seemed lost can hardly be overestimated. During the Commonwealth, Henry Hammond's *Practical Catechism* (1644) William Nicholson's *Plain and Full Exposition of the Catechism* (1655) and Richard Sherlock's *The Catechism of the Church of England Explained* (1656) appeared. It was the time when John Evelyn complained that no real Christian instruction was being given in the parish churches – 'there was now nothing practical preached, or that pressed for reformation of life, but high and speculative points and straines . . . which left people very ignorant and of no steady principles'.[40] Nicholson objected that 'sermonising hath justled out this necessary instruction'.[41] In *The Golden Grove* which really started out as such an exposition, Taylor offers his book as an alternative to the view of those who had destroyed the Church that 'all religion is a sermon'.[42] After the Restoration, and for a different set of reasons, there was an equal need for such handbooks of faith and practice, and Thomas Ken's *Exposition of the Church Catechism* appeared in 1685 and William Beveridge published his *The Church Catechism Explained* in 1704. Towards the close of the eighteenth century Isaac Mann, Bishop of Cork (1772–1789) produced a late example, his *Familiar Exposition of the Church Catechism*. Probably the earliest example of the genre even though it was a posthumous publication in 1630 is Lancelot Andrewes's *Pattern of Catechistical Doctrine*.

This kind of book then made a substantial contribution to the Anglican heritage both in theology and spirituality. The usual layout following that of the Catechism is an exposition of the creed, the Lord's prayer or prayer generally, and the sacraments, followed by an explanation of the decalogue and the duties. The objective was to create a generation 'steadfast in the Faith and sincere in their obedience',[43] through instruction in the apostolic doctrine, through the breaking of bread and the prayers, through character-building by grace in a workaday world where men and women are called to 'the new life'. The current of 'practical divinity' runs as strongly in these books as it does in the literature of Anglican spirituality as a whole. Although Parts I and II of Andrewes's *Pattern* deal with doctrine, Part III, the largest, develops the law of Christ from the decalogue. The now familiar threefold structure of the duties, 'piously, soberly and justly' includes faith, hope and love, humility, zeal and perseverance, prayer and the use of the liturgy. The root sins and their causes and consequences are analysed. Discipline and the details of the duties proper to different callings are examined. Moral/ascetical theology is at work in the pastoral and parochial setting but always the end is kept in view, as in Nicholson's *Exposition*: grace is for 'those who are born again, sanctified by the Spirit of God, cleansed by Christ's blood, engraffed and made *partakers of the Divine Nature*'. Grace, he writes, does not raise man to 'an unsinning obedience, but it makes him a *new creature*, creates in him a *sincere obedience* to the whole Gospel'.[44] The structure of all these manuals is virtually the same being dictated by the form and content of the Catechism but the handling of the subjects and their range differ with the various writers. Hammond, for example, includes material on divorce, usury, sacrilege and even duels. His *Practical Catechism* (1644) was popular enough to go into many editions and Charles I admired it greatly.

The catechetical books belong to what I have ventured to characterize as the Anglican spirituality of the Five D's, devotion, duty, discipline, detail and doctrine. By their combination of devotion and practicality, their awareness of the range of human problems and of the need to apply Christian standards in and to society, *they act as an image converter for this spirituality* on the screen of personal and daily experience. No assessment of Caroline religious practice can afford to ignore the extent and the depth of their influence. Their simplicity and realism lent thrust to the concept of membership the goal of which was that men 'may the more expeditely follow Christ'.[45]

This sketch of our Anglican heritage is done and at the end one is more conscious than ever that it is at best but an impression so rich is the picture of what we have inherited from those who have gone before us. For many people the past is another country. It need not be so when it is our own past. As we begin to penetrate it, our past is seen to be indispensably a creative part of our present. We come to realize that it is not another country but our *patria*, our homeland and the place of our origins, which under God has made us what we are.

6

Postscript from the Present

*'Christ is whole with the whole Church, and whole with
every part of the Church, as touching his Person'*
— Richard Hooker

I

WE have heard voices speaking to us from our own past, but
what about the present and the future? I deprecate the suggestion
current in some circles ever since Lambeth 1930 that the
vocation of Anglicanism is to disappear once unity has been
achieved. It would seem to me to have all the appearance of
loose talk arising from a position not thought-through and
from a deficient concept of Christian unity. The notion is
invalid and untrue not only because it appears to imply a
concealed identification of unity with uniformity but because
it misses the point that any unity worth having will be rich
with all the treasures of the uniting Churches. To say this is
to do more than fall back on another of the current phrases,
though one better based, 'unity in diversity'. Too often this
has been used either as a bromide or as a talisman. What a
unity brought about by the Spirit abiding in the Church must
surely mean is that the coming Great Church will embody *the
best of ourselves* as the gift which each tradition can bring to
Christ who prayed that they may be one in Him. The best
that Anglicanism, Methodism or Roman Catholicism has
learnt and acquired through the centuries as each tradition
has striven through grace to proclaim and to live 'the gospel
of God', this is what each brings as an offering.

We shall not be expected to pretend that *our* past never
happened or is irrelevant or that it has never been creative in
our present. Rather shall we be expected to bring it as a gift
to enrich the continuing life of the *Ecumene*; not as something

we created but which created us; not as something to be defended at all costs but as a contribution to the shared mission of the *koinonia*, a gift with no strings attached. True unity must involve pooling spiritual resources. If some prove to be less serviceable than others, less expressive of authentic Christian believing and behaving, then the consensus of the faithful will make this evident as the tradition of a united Church develops under the Spirit's imperative and under the check of God's Word of which the Church is both witness and keeper. No doubt *some* aspects of *all* our traditions must indeed go but the best, *each tradition at its best*, must remain. Only the winnowing experience of living and worshipping together in the unity of the future will decide: 'For no one can lay any foundation other than the one already laid, which is Jesus Christ. If any man builds on this foundation using gold, silver, costly stones, wood, hay or straw, his work will be shown for what it is, because the Day will bring it to light'. (1 Cor.3.12).

To think in these terms is not to indulge in a sort of ecclesial day-dreaming. There are facts and factors which point in this direction. There is the Bonn Agreement of 1931 between Anglicans and Old Catholics which provides that:

(1) Each Communion recognises the catholicity and independence of the other, and maintains it own.
(2) Each Communion agrees to admit members of the other Communion to participate in the sacraments.
(3) Intercommunion does not require from either Communion the acceptance of all doctrinal opinion, sacramental devotion, or liturgical practice characteristic of the other, but implies that each believes the other to hold all the essentials of the Christian Faith.

This is an agreement for *full intercommunion* but more interesting still because of its direct bearing on the concept of unity we have been visualizing is the status of the Uniat Churches in communion with Rome. An observer has commented that previously they were only 'rites' but at Vatican II it was discovered that they were Churches, preserving their own patrimony of liturgy and spirituality in *full communion*.

Nor can we forget words used by Pope Paul VI in St Peter's Basilica in 1970 which were a turning-point and which were welcomed by the 100th Archbishop of Canterbury:

'There will be no seeking to lessen the legitimate prestige and the worthy patrimony of piety and usage proper to the Anglican Church when the Roman Catholic Church – this humble 'Servant of the servants of God' – is able to embrace her ever beloved sister in the one authentic Communion of the family of Christ: a communion of origin and faith, a communion of priesthood and rule, a communion of the saints in the freedom and love of the spirit of Jesus. Perhaps we shall have to go on, waiting and watching in prayer, in order to deserve that blessed day'.

Commenting on the words, Robert Hale wrote: 'Such a distinct identity and heritage constitute a Church, and also ground its right to a distinctive place in the eventual communion of Churches which is the objective of the ecumenical movement'.[1] What in fact we are talking about is a communion of Communions, collegial communion as Robert Adolfs put it. This is brought squarely into the present by the agreed statement *Church as Communion* (1991) of ARCIC II. Assuming that by 'ecclesial communion' and 'the communion of all the churches' is meant and implied much the same as 'a communion of communions', there is much that is supportive of the position that, in the sharing of gifts, ecclesial identities in fact make a major contribution to the *Ecumene*. Moreover, while affirming that varieties complement one another and that diversity does not lead to division (36), the statement firmly underlines the central role of the *hapax*: 'Diversity of cultures may often elicit a diversity in the expression of the one Gospel; within the same community distinct perceptions and practices arise. Nevertheless these must remain faithful to the tradition received from the apostles (cf. Jude 3)', (29) and cf. (53). This is filled out in the definition of the necessary elements of ecclesial communion: 'It is now possible to describe what constitutes ecclesial communion. It is rooted in the confession of the one apostolic faith, revealed in the Scriptures, and set forth in the Creeds. It is founded upon one baptism. The one celebration of the eucharist is its pre-eminent expression and focus' (45).

Following on from this is the Commission's description of 'a communion' and of 'being in communion': 'For a local community to be *a communion* means that it is a gathering of the baptised brought together by the apostolic preaching, confessing the one faith, celebrating the one eucharist, and led by an apostolic ministry. This implies that this local church is in communion with all Christian communities in which the essential constitutive elements of ecclesial life are present. For all the local churches to be *together in communion*, the one visible communion which God wills, it is required that all the essential elements of ecclesial communion are present and mutually recognised in each of them. Thus the visible communion between these churches is complete and their ministers are in communion with each other. This does not necessitate precisely the same canonical ordering: diversity of canonical structures is part of the acceptable diversity which enriches the one communion of all the churches' (43). In other words, the complementarity and mutual enrichment of the traditions rather than the submerging of ecclesial identities is seen as a fruitful element in growing towards 'fuller communion'.

This scenario represents the ideal but in the actual inter-Church situation the crunch comes when articles which are not agreed as belonging to the foundation are advanced as part of 'the essential constitutive elements of ecclesial life' and made necessary for complete communion: or when a development is claimed to be legitimate and consonant with the Gospel and tradition but not so agreed by both participants in the dialogue. Precisely these points are made in general terms, as we shall note, by Bramhall and Küng in their different settings, situations and affiliation. It is extremely difficult to visualise any solution capable of becoming actual which does not involve a joint and rigorous use and application of the fundamentals/secondaries distinction and/or of the hierarchy of truths.

The agreed statement's welcome references to 'separated

churches growing towards ecclesial communion' and 'moving forward together towards visible unity and ecclesial communion' together with the use of such terms as degrees and dimensions of communion are not to be regarded as vague and pious aspirations. To be effectual they will realistically imply a process of unity by stages. The concept envisages a *growth-process* in which, at each stage, a new inter-Church relationship commensurate with the degree of agreement then reached is institutionally established between the Churches. Into that process there have already entered two working principles, mainly as a result of inter-Church dialogue in recent years, principles which because of their realism are of the greatest importance as instruments for achieving advance that is genuine and not fudged agreement. *The first is the concept of substantial agreement and the second is the concept of convergence.* Both take for granted that each Church in the dialogue has an identity which must be brought alongside of the other Church's identity as both 'listen to each other and jointly return to the primary sources', to quote the *Lima Report* of the World Council of Churches.[2] In fact, those who have worked at the coalface of Christian unity have soon discovered the paradox that the more truly they can express in love their own tradition at its richest the better they are able to understand in depth and to value the other tradition with which they are in dialogue. Confrontational attitudes dissolve and each begins to glimpse his own Church reflected in the face of his neighbour's Church. Some would say that this could be the Spirit's way of solving our problems of identity and could be a gage of what might happen in a Church united. Be that as it may, the experience is a real one and has its bearing on the supposed disappearance of our distinctive traditions into the anonymity of some sort of ecclesial amalgam.

Substantial agreement as a term in inter-Church dialogue made its first modest appearance at the Malines Conversations (1921–1925).[3] Already, unity by convergence, unity in diversity, sufficient agreement, had surfaced at the meetings and Bishop Gore for the Anglicans insisted that 'the demand for the distinction between fundamentals and non-fundamentals will go on'.[4] In our day, substantial agreement is a major factor in the *Final Report* (ARCIC I) and in the *Lima Report*.[5] The purpose of the term is to show that a *real* agreement exists which is not a *full* agreement. It has nothing to do with finding the lowest common denominator. Rather is it, as J. M. R. Tillard has pointed out, 'a search for what pertains to the essence, and according to which, *in diverse forms, the two traditions live*'.[6] It means that those in dialogue agree on 'the same substantial data of faith' which in the two traditions have been drawn out into a divergent theology and practice. In other words – and this is the point I have been making about the non-absorption of one ecclesial identity by the other or the absorption of both together in some undefined totality – the distinction recognises the existence of the different ecclesial traditions as something real and valuable but insists that where there is substantial agreement there exists 'a deep agreement on what could be called the axis of faith'.

The principle of unity by convergence can be seen at work during the second decade of the eighteenth century in the correspondence between William Wake, Archbishop of Canterbury, and the French Roman Catholic theologians, Girardin, Du Pin and Le Courayer. The circumstances of the times prevented the concept from spilling over into the workshops of a dialogue, but it was to the fore as an objective at Malines. W. H. Frere for the Anglicans spoke at the first meeting advising that instead of the old confrontational route each Church should head towards unity *'par une marche en avant convergente'*.[7] For the Roman Catholics a paper was read which chimed with this principle. This was Dom Lambert Beauduin's 'L'Église Anglicane unie non absorbée'. Here in another form is the theme of Churches preserving their proper patrimony, themselves at their best, within a communion of Communions. In 1960, Archbishop Fisher of Canterbury in conversation with Pope John XXIII made the same point which Frere had made, 'We are looking forward until, in God's good time, our two courses approximate and meet'. To which the Pope replied, 'You are right'.[8]

Henceforward, the concept has become an ecumenical commonplace. We meet it in the *Malta Report* (1968), in the *Common Declaration* (1977) of the Pope and the Archbishop of Canterbury, and it is a governing concept in the *Final Report* (1982) and in the *Lima Report* (1982).

The fundamentals of the Faith are non-negotiable. The *Malta Report* (3) makes this clear and goes on to explain how the ethos of a particular Church is created by the way in which it receives and expresses the inheritance of faith: 'Divergences since the sixteenth century have arisen not so much from the substance of this inheritance *as from our separate ways of receiving it*. They derive from our experience of its value and power, from our interpretation of its meaning and authority, from our formulation of its content, from our theological elaboration of what it implies, and from our understanding of the manner in which the Church should keep and teach the Faith'.(4)

II

Seen within this wider context of separated Churches seeking unity in truth, Anglicanism's ethos with its insistence on 'the faith once for all delivered' and on the distinction between fundamentals and secondary truths, its understanding of living tradition in relation to the primacy of Scripture and its assertion of the freedom of intellectual enquiry, is of extreme relevance. It is relevant not only in respect of Anglican identity but because it can be of major service in the quest for unity. It was a Roman Catholic, Van de Pol, who wrote 'All Anglican Churches, however,. are one in their conscious endeavour to preserve the apostolic faith and character of the church's worship of the first centuries, though trying to incorporate in it the contributions of the Reformation and those of their own time so far as they have positive and permanent value. This typical Anglican attitude in respect of tradition and enrichment is at the basis of the moderation and comprehensiveness of Anglicanism. It marks world-Anglicanism as being, as it were, a provisional proto-type of the reunited *Ecumene*, the world Christianity of the future'.[9] That was well said and it underlines from a fresh stand-point the theme suggested in this postscript, that far from having a vocation to disappear Anglicanism has a vocation of responsibility to be its best self and not for its own sake only but for the sake of the Church which is to be, *out and 'beyond where any of the present Churches are at the present time'*.[10] The phrase is Michael Marshall's and it suggests that in the long view (the Spirit's view?) being true to its own best self-understanding is the main contribution Anglicanism can make to the unity of Christians. Provided we realise in fraternal love that our fellow-Christians of other traditions are feeling and doing the same, then the vision of the *Una Sancta* in all its fulness, grown somewhat misty in recent years, can shine with a new brightness.

Thirty years ago the same conviction impelled Archbishop Michael Ramsey to claim that 'the times call urgently for the Anglican witness to Scripture, tradition and reason – alike for meeting the problems which Biblical theology is creating, *for serving the reintegration of the Church*, and for presenting the faith as at once supernatural and related to contemporary man'.[11] He forcibly reiterated this conviction with particular emphasis on the role of the threefold appeal and of the continuing Anglican identity in respect of unity in lectures given at Nashotah House, Wisconsin, in 1979 and now published for the first time (Michael Ramsey, *The Anglican Spirit*, SPCK 1991, ed. Dale Coleman). Obviously, like Van de Pol and Marshall, he sees the Anglican identity as precious in and for itself and potentially so in the quest for unity. *The question today is whether that threefold appeal is as effective and as serviceable* as it was reckoned to be by the great phalanx of Anglican theologians of the seventeenth century to whose work it was basic and foundational. In our age the critical element in all theology from biblical studies and the study of the evolution of doctrine to the impact of psychological and medical research on moral theology is far more marked and advanced. Yet it may well be that we can get the perspective somewhat out of focus here if we think of the Caroline divines as handling the threefold appeal simplistically. What P. E. More once wrote about seventeenth-century Anglican theology holds good: 'What we have to look for . . . is not so much finality as direction'. The Carolines were clear as to the direction. They were unanimously bent on establishing from the evidence that the Church of England was in direct continuity of faith and order with the Primitive Church. The appeal to Scripture, to tradition and to reason established for them the continued and continuing profession of the original, authentic Christian faith and practice by means of the only valid criteria available to men. Is not this precisely how Van de Pol sees the Anglican ethos operating today?

III

As to the mechanics of the threefold appeal they did not use it as a sort of blanket guarantor and they were aware of tensions in the interface of the elements in the appeal while totally convinced that it was the only way of maintaining the Church in the truth of the faith once for all delivered. Naturally and inevitably the contemporary level of hermeneutics is reflected in their attitude to the text and authority of the Scriptures. Nevertheless, Browne can see the creation-narrative as an allegory and Robert Boyle is at pains to stress that not everything in Scripture is Scripture and that the Bible is an assembled divine library: 'We should carefully distinguish betwixt what the Scripture itself says and what is only said in the Scripture. For we must not look on the Bible as an oration of God to men, or as a body of laws like our English Statute Book . . . but as a collection of composures of very differing sorts and written at very distant times'. Yet, the authors 'were acted by the Holy Spirit, who both excited and assisted them in penning the Scriptures'.[12] Laud may believe that Matthew wrote the first Gospel but he is aware that 'The credit of Scripture to be Divine resolves finally into that faith which we have touching God himself'. He distinguishes between the principle that Scripture is the Word of God and 'all other necessary points of Divinity' because the latter are inferred from Scripture itself but the former 'is grounded on no compelling or demonstrative ratiocination, but relies upon the strength of faith'. If a man doubts the 'infallible verity' of Scripture 'the world cannot keep him from going to weigh it at the balance of reason, whether it be the Word of God or not . . . and in all this there is no harm. The danger is when a man will use no other scale but reason . . . For the Word of God, and the Book containing it, refuse not to be weighed by reason. But the scale is not large enough to contain . . . the true virtue and full force of either'. Laud is vividly aware of both the supportive cohesion and the tensive interaction of the three elements in the appeal: 'I admit no ordinary rule left now in the Church, of divine and infallible verity, and so of faith, but the Scripture. And I believe the entire Scripture, first, by the tradition of the Church; then, *by all other credible motives* . . . and last of all, by the light which shines in Scripture itself, kindled in believers by the Spirit of God. Then, I believe the entire Scripture infallibly, and by a divine infallibility am sure of my object. Then am I as sure of my believing, which is the act of my faith, conversant about this object: for no man believes, but he must needs know in himself whether he believes or no, and wherein and how he doubts. Then I am infallibly assured of my Creed, *the tradition of the Church inducing, and the Scripture confirming it*. And I believe both Scripture and Creed in the same uncorrupted sense which the primitive Church believed them; and am sure that I do so believe them, because I cross not in my belief anything delivered by the primitive Church. And this, again, I am sure of because I take the belief of the primitive Church, as it is expressed and delivered by the Councils and ancient Fathers of those times'.[13] Here is an affirmation of faith in which can be seen the function and working of the appeal which has been of the essence of Anglican identity. Laud was indeed writing for a whole Church.

That these were times of intellectual transition is clear from Edward Stillingfleet's *Origines Sacrae* (1662) which sets out to be 'a rational account' of Christian belief concerning the truth of the Scriptures and their 'divine authority'. It is a remarkable blend of insistence on the Mosaic authorship and on the historicity of Adam with awareness of the implications of contemporary science and philosophy – Ray and Descartes are mentioned. He faces 'the most popular pretences of the atheists of our age' who claim 'the irreconcilableness of the account of times in Scripture with that of the learned and ancient heathen nations; the inconsistency of the belief of the Scriptures with the principles of reason; and the account which may be given of the origin of things from principles of philosophy (i.e. 'science') without the Scriptures'.[14] Influenced by Henry More and determined to proclaim Christianity as a faith which modern men can with integrity embrace, the constant setting of his argument continues as we have seen it to be 'Scripture, reason, or the consent of the Primitive Church'.[15] Stillingfleet is thoroughly at home in patristic studies but *critically* so: 'It is not enough to prove that one or two Fathers did speak something tending to it, but that all who had occasion to mention it, did speak of it as the doctrine of the Church'.[16] 'Without the rational inducements which do incline the mind to a firm assent' faith would be 'an unaccountable thing . . . and the spirit of revelation would not be the spirit of wisdom'. The upshot, says Stillingfleet, would be that 'religion would be exposed to the contempt of all unbelievers'.[17] He regards the creed as a *condensing* of fundamentals and 'the creed must suppose the Scripture'.[18] Here is someone acutely alive to the problems of faith and reason in a fast-changing intellectual climate but who can see no sounder approach than that of the threefold appeal; 'and next to Scripture and reason, I attribute so much to *the sense of* the Christian Church in the ages next succeeding the apostles'.[19]

The famous preacher, John Tillotson, who became Archbishop of Canterbury in 1691, presents us with the same approach: 'reason is the faculty whereby revelation is to be discerned'.[20] Preached to an educated congregation at St Laurence, Jewry, his sermons aim at nourishing the practice of religion and insist that the condition of justification is 'faith perfected by charity'.[21] He rejects teaching about reprobation and assurance and insists that theology must be about *meanings*, not terminology, and 'it does not alter the case to give reason ill names'.[22] Burnet said that 'the nation proposed him as a pattern'.

Daniel Whitby in 1666 put it this way, 'Reason in judging the sense of Scripture is regulated partly by principles of Faith, partly by Tradition, partly by Catholic maxims of her own'.[23] The more one ponders that definition the more one realises that far from being simplistic it is both flexible and profound. We can detect in it a foreshadowing of the 'mutual support' and checking, the 'suppleness and elasticity', which Lambeth 1948 saw in the organically related elements in the Anglican identity. Whitby entered the lists against John Sergeant, the controversialist which whom Jeremy Taylor crossed swords. There is no more consistent and candid user of this theological method than Taylor himself for whose work it is always explicitly the basis. Yet he uses it with the sensitivity of an orthodox theologian who understands the complexities of belief and behaviour and in whose make-up there is an individual strain of liberality and a strong feeling for intellectual freedom. His friend Rust spoke of Taylor's 'largeness and freedom of spirit' and in an age when some were dogmatic about everything he is prepared to say 'We do not know', 'Beyond this we can do no more'. Though 'the revelation' controls his thinking he goes deep into the faith and reason debate concluding that 'always our reason (such as it is) must lead us into such proportions of faith as they can'.[24] We have seen in the first chapter something of what he understands by reason as distinct from the reasoning process and there is kinship here with, and very likely an influence from, the Cambridge Platonists. Whichcote's strangely modern pupil John Smith maintained that divinity is a divine life rather than a divine science, not an 'art' but a 'living form'. Truth and wisdom, he contends, are not *only* concerned with rationality: 'It is only Life that can feelingly converse with life'. As faith turns into vision, reason, from being a discursive faculty becomes 'a serene understanding . . . an intellectual calmness'. Reason in man, says Smith, is *'lumen de lumine'* but its inward virtue is damaged by the Fall and so revealed truth is required to help us to understand what God is like and 'to work out all those notions of God which are the true ground-work of love and obedience to God, and conformity to him'. To understand what Scripture is means realising that the Gospel is 'something more than a piece of book-learning or an historical narration'. The Gospel is 'a vital form and principle', 'a vital quickening thing' and the new law is not rules and regulations but 'an efflux of life' and 'produceth life'.[25] And did not Taylor in one of his greatest sermons, *Via Intelligentiae*, write 'theology is rather a divine life than a divine knowledge'?

With Taylor and Smith we have moved into a religious world in which dogma is not an all-embracing end in itself or a *ne plus ultra* inscribed on the theological Pillars of Hercules, but *a necessary fence* about the truth which has within it endless subtleties and variations of expression. The *hapax* is there and so is 'the candle of the Lord'.

Jeremy Taylor was possibly the most original theologian of the period and this quality affected much of his huge output from the reform of moral theology through his devotional and eucharistic writings to his general theological synthesis. Just when he appears to belong to his own times he steps into ours. Like the great majority of his contempor-aries he accepts the historicity of Adam and the Fall but at once he refuses to accept the current theological deductions from it. Original sin does *not* make us heirs of damnation and in us is simply 'a contagion'. It has neither impaired our choice nor determined sinning in us: 'Adam had liberty of choice and chose ill and so do we'; 'Could we prevent the sin of Adam? Could we hinder it? *Were we ever asked?*'[26] All the time, Taylor consciously works at his theology in the context of Scripture and tradition but always independently and critically and allowing its due freedom to reason for 'into the greatest mysteriousness of our religion, and the deepest articles of faith, we enter by reason'.[27] It is along these lines that he approaches the exposition of Scripture in *A Discourse of the Liberty of Prophesying* (1647). He sees that there is difficulty in expounding Scripture and therefore since 'We must hope to be saved in the belief of things plain, necessary and fundamental, and our pious endeavour to find out God's meaning in such places, which he hath left under a cloud for other great ends reserved to his own knowledge, we shall see a very great necessity in allowing a liberty in prophesying'.[28] There are so many ways of interpreting Scripture 'in questions controverted' such as 'searching the originals, conference of places, parity of reason, and analogy of faith, which are all dubious, uncertain, and very fallible'. Such 'matters of question' (Taylor means non-fundamentals) are further complicated by 'so many copies (of the text of Scripture) with infinite varieties of reading' and by the fact that some passages can have different literal meanings, and others spiritual meanings and so on. In these areas of Scripture-interpretation he concludes that every man should have liberty, and as for fundamentals, 'Holy Scripture is the repository of divine truths, and the great rule of faith' and the Creed summarizes 'all that which is of simple and prime necessity'.[29] He then submits to analysis the question whether tradition is certain enough and sufficient to decide such controverted matters, finding that the variety and uncertainty of traditions and rites, the origins of some and the falling into disuse of others, disqualify such a solution. Taylor thinks better of Councils though he knows no reason 'that they shall be absolutely assisted . . . whether they will or no: faith is a virtue as well as charity and therefore consists in liberty and choice, and hath nothing in it of necessity . . . neither did any general council ever offer a decree which *they did not think sufficiently proved by Scripture, reason, or tradition*, as appears in the acts of the councils'.[30] After looking at the decisions, activities and records of various General Councils his judgement is that 'they are excellent instruments of peace, the best human judicatories in the world . . . and the greatest probability from human authority' nevertheless beyond this and 'besides these advantages . . . I know nothing greater that general councils can pretend to with reason and argument sufficient to satisfy any wise man'. Their authority is neither infallible nor unlimited,

'They made nothing true that was not so before', but they are 'excellent guides' where there is no argument of greater force than their decrees.[31]

The general Anglican attitude to the Fathers is one almost of veneration bound up as it was with their claim to continuity with what Jewel called the Church of 'the Apostles and old Catholic Fathers'. Nevertheless it is a critical veneration and Taylor who makes great use of patristics in many of his books does so critically. He was influenced in this respect, as were the members of the Tew Circle, by Daillé's book *Du Vrai Usage des Pères* (1632). This work set out to show that a fixed criterion could not be expected from antiquity because of differences among the Fathers and because of the early appearance of doctrinal divergences in the patristic period. The Anglican appeal to antiquity however did not suffer much as a method from the emergence of the critical study of the Fathers in which in point of fact Anglicans such as Sir Henry Savile, Patrick Young and Primate Ussher had distinguished themselves early in the century. The reason was that the appeal to antiquity and to the Fathers was identity-confirming and faith-affirming. Again, it is a question of direction and for the Anglicans the appeal to antiquity is always confirmatory of the appeal to Scripture: Jeremy Taylor was vastly learned in patristics and he speaks for all when he says that the whole point of appealing to the Fathers is to show that 'when the Fathers appeal to tradition . . . it is such a tradition as delivers the fundamental points of Christianity, which were also recorded in Scripture'. They acquit us 'from any other necessity of believing than of such articles as are recorded in Scripture', and thus our identity with them is confirmed.[32] In the General Dedication to *Episcopacy Asserted* and *Authorized and Set Forms of Liturgy* Taylor sets out a measured and balanced assessment of how the appeal to tradition and the Fathers can help in establishing the authenticity of Christian believing.[33]

The fact is that even members of the Tew Circle such as Chillingworth did not abandon the appeal to tradition though they modified it and were criticial in their use of the Fathers insisting that they could not be treated as a certain standard of reference though in fact Anglicanism had never so regarded them. Yet Chillingworth was explicit in his agreement that Anglican faith and practice are consonant with antiquity. John Hales, 'the ever memorable', for whom tradition was the weakest member of the triad wrote 'For it is not depth of knowledge, nor knowledge of antiquity, or sharpness of wit, nor authority of councils, nor the name of the Church, can settle the restless conceits that possess the minds of many doubtful Christians: only to ground for Faith on the plain uncontroversable text of Scripture'. In the same sermon which is about 'abuses of hard places of Scripture' he affirms that 'the interpreters of our own times, because of their skill in the original languages . . . have generally surpassed the best of the ancients'. His nod in the direction of the Fathers, though he has just quoted St Basil approvingly, is perfunctory: 'Which I speak not to discountenance antiquity, but that all ages, all persons may have their due'.[34] Chillingworth was indebted to Hales who like Taylor had been chaplain to Laud who was Chillingworth's god-father.

Looking back over our investigations up to this point, it seems clear that, by way of contrast to Lord Macaulay, Mr Gladstone was correct when he said to Morley: 'Do you know whom I find the most tolerant Churchman of that time? Laud! Laud got Davenant made Bishop of Salisbury, and he zealously befriended Chillingworth and Hales'.[35] He could have added that a perusal of the *Conference* would have reinforced his conclusion. The last word here should be Jeremy Taylor's: 'Scripture, tradition, councils, and fathers, are the evidence in a question, but reason is the judge'.[36]

Having listened to these voices from our past I venture to think that it is a fair assessment to judge that seventeenth-century Anglican theologians did not use the threefold appeal like the Stamp Act of 1765 to guarantee by a cursory reference to origins the authenticity of this or that article of belief or doctrinal formulation. Rather, within the given limitations of the scholarship and the knowledge of their times, did they apply the criteria with sensitivity, honesty, and freedom, and in some cases, with a surprising modernity. No review of how they went about it could fairly describe their procedure as simplistic. Is is possible for us in our situation to do the same, given a changed perspective in society and in scholarship? Was Archbishop Ramsey's a valid evaluation or was he being too optimistic?

IV

'It is commonly said that the Anglicans base their perception of Christian truth on Scripture, Tradition and Reason. But this threefold dialectic is beginning to look like a methodological strait-jacket for a Church which no longer actually lives in it.' My contention is that it never was and need not now be a strait-jacket and that the use of the appeal and, equally important, its direction are still valid not only for Anglican identity but as a valuable instrument in ecumenical dialogue. I would suggest that the evidence selected for this postscript indicates that in the past, given the circumstances of the time, Anglicans moved with a degree of freedom and a strong sense of direction within the operation of the threefold dialectic. I would hope to give some reasons for believing that they can and should continue to do so now and in the future. But first, the sentence comes from an article in *Theology* for March/ April 1990 by one of the editors Peter Coleman. The article, headed 'The Price is Still to be Paid' is concerned with the ordination of women and the extract quoted above continues: 'There are at least four components which need reconciling in the Anglican Communion at the moment. Tradition actually means that point in development now reached by the Western Catholic Church. This tradition can change abruptly, as with its vernacular liturgy, so it is not necessarily preservative. Scripture means careful attention to the biblical texts, with exegesis and hermeneutics taken seriously, and is by no means confined to fundamentalism. Reason among Anglicans no longer means building the kind of logical structure of doctrine and ethics from certain clear bases that was still possible, say, in the days of Bicknell's *Thirty-nine Articles* (1919). It means estimating continually the God-given value of experience, and not merely following the spirit of the age'. It is not fanciful to picture Boyle, Wilkins, Taylor, Chillingworth, Smith and their fellows reading this, nodding in agreement and saying 'But please, within the stock of ideas and information available to us, this is what we were saying!' Coleman's assessment would certainly seem an acceptable one to me though I do not think that it validates either in the past or in the present a concept of the threefold dialectic as a methodological strait-jacket. I would agree too with what he goes on to say about the need for a component which he labels as 'spontaneity' by which he means 'that apostolic sense of the immediate interaction between God's people and his Spirit'. He is surely right when he says 'the freedom of God's people to be spontaneous in what they sense ought to be done now is a permanent element of the Christian tradition'.[37] To be alive to changing perceptions of what is right for the Church and to be critically sensitive to the unprecedented situation which may possibly be a *kairos*, a time of fulfilment, must always be an option for those who believe that the Church is the Spirit-filled Body.

In the present situation of theology and in the context of separated Christians seeking to recover unity, I would suggest that Anglicanism's vocation of responsibility to others and to itself involves maintaining its threefold dialectic as a necessary ecumenical methodology and for the following reasons. In the first place, it is our insurance against a blindfold Christianity with earplugs. At the moment, and in more than one Church, a confident Christianity can be undermined by either or both of two trends. There is a fundamentalism of Scripture, a literalist interpretation of that which is seen by all as normative for the Church. There is also a fundamentalism of tradition which sees it much as a fly-in-amber rather than the living Church interpreting 'the faith once for all delivered' in the idiom and the life-setting of each generation. By way of illustration, just as this postscript was being written, the Church Society, through the chairman of its council, is reported as faulting the Doctrine Commission's new report on the Holy Spirit by asserting that it displays 'an ambivalent attitude' to the authority of Scripture. If the newspaper account is correct, the chairman is reported as saying that Bible-believing Christians will find it difficult to accept baptism described as 'a declarative legal act'; Christ spoken of as 'made present through the bread and wine'; condemnation of the Old Testament prohibition of images; the assumption of biological evolution; and the undermining of the doctrine of everlasting punishment of the wicked.[38] At the same time we note in Hans Küng's recent book *Reforming the Church Today* (1990) that he sees a future for the Church only if it is connected to its origins and to the present and not 'infatuated with the past'. One of the three conditions under which he sees the Church having a future is 'If it preserves the *great Catholic tradition* supported by the Gospel (but not the many little Catholic traditions that are by no means always supported by the Gospel)'[39] In both cases, the relevance of insistence on the *hapax* and of the threefold appeal can hardly be in question. *How right Jeremy Taylor was.* Clearly, the danger from which the traditional Anglican dialectic preserves the Church is that of turning the appeal into a duet or even a solo instead of a trio, elbowing out reason and giving it ill names, to quote Tillotson.

Furthermore, the matter of the continuity of doctrine cannot be evaded simply because the demands 'How do I know that this is authentic, original Christianity?' and 'Where is genuine doctrine to be found?' are even more pressing now than in the seventeenth century. Only such a method as the threefold appeal ensures this continuity together with freedom in assessing the answers given to those questions.

For much the same reasons, the question of direction remains vitally important. To quote Küng again, the Church has a future 'if it reflects on its *origin* and continually reorients itself to the gospel, to Jesus Christ himself'. One is reminded of John Pearson's *Exposition of the Creed* (1659): 'The only way to attain unto the knowledge of the true notion of the Church, is to search into the New Testament, and from the places there which mention it, to conclude what is the nature of it'. For the threefold appeal a positive choice of direction is intrinsic and tradition is evaluated by its adherence to the original 'deposit of faith'. Within this process, the freedom to weigh the evidence is an essential element.

That all this is of the Anglican identity is obvious but that it impinges on participation in unity conversations and in agreed statements is also self-evident. It is because of this undifferentiated Catholicism that there is nothing contradictory in being robustly Anglican and robustly ecumenical at the same time. It was Archbishop Benson of Canterbury, speaking at Kildare Cathedral in Ireland in 1896, who said 'Our Church no more sought a *via media* between Rome and Geneva than St George's Channel invented a *via media* between England and Ireland. Our Church created no new fictitious platform of authority. It was, and it relied upon itself as, the ancient Catholic Church'. What he is in fact doing is stating the *hapax* in the ecclesial context as did his predecessors from Jewel through Laud, Beveridge, Taylor and Bramhall, to mention but a few. Bramhall spelt it out with its implications for continuity of doctrine; we adhere to 'the authority of the primitive fathers and the General Councils', to 'the old faith of the whole Christian world, that is the creed of the apostles, explicated by the Nicene, Constantinopolitan, Ephesine, and Chalcedonian fathers'. Moreover, he sees the implications for the reintegration of the Christian Church; the causes of separation are 'new articles of faith', equating 'opinions with fundamental truths', 'excluding all the rest of the Christian world by new doctrines'. He takes the same simple and positive position as Benson; it is 'separation from the pure primitive Church which produced the second separation'. His conclusion is the same: 'Our religion is the same it was, our Church the same it was, our Holy Orders the same they were' and the criterion is 'the infallible rule of faith, that is, the Holy Scriptures, interpreted by the Catholic Church'.[40] The ecumenical encounter is thus having to take account of the presence of a Church which has no dogmas which is regards as essential characteristics of its identity and which sees itself simply as the Catholic Church committed only to the Catholic faith of the New Testament and the Creeds. Bramhall and Benson saw the ecumenical implications of this Anglican identity and we are again reminded of Van de Pol's comments. As Gore pointed out at Malines it seems likely that separated Christians will yet rediscover that the only route out of the *impasse* is by way of the classical Anglican fundamentals/secondaries distinction. That this is more than merely hopeful thinking is indicated by the recent publication of a study document on '*The Notion of "Hierarchy of Truths" – An Ecumenical Interpretation*'. The work on the document was jointly organized by the Pontifical Council for Promoting Christian Unity and the Secretariat of the Commission on Faith and Order of the World Council of Churches. Bearing in mind the resemblances we detected earlier between the two principles we can only be encouraged by such passages as the following: 'An appreciation of "hierarchy of truths" could mean that the ecumenical agenda will be based upon a *communion in the "foundation" that already exists* and will point the way to that ordering of priorities which makes possible a *gradual growth* into full communion' (34), and 'By better understanding *the ways in which other Christians hold, express and live the faith*, each confessional tradition is often led *to a better understanding also of itself*, and can begin to see its own formulations of doctrine in a broader perspective. This experience and discernment of each other is *mutually enriching* . . . The process is a means of more adequately assessing expressions of the truth of revelation, their interrelation, their necessity and the possible diversity of formulations. *Refocussing on the "foundation"*, a hierarchy of truths may therefore be an instrument of that theological and spiritual renewal which the ecumenical movement requires' (36).[41]

In both these extracts the luxury of italics has been indulged in because of the striking way in which the study-document reinforces some of the major conclusions which we have been advancing here.

There could hardly be a more fitting way of rounding off this postscript than by directing attention to *The Continuity of Christian Doctrine* (1981) by the late R. P. C. Hanson in whose distinguished writings over the last half-century the threefold appeal is alive and well. In his Tuohy Lectures we find an estimate which coincides with the position here set out. Hanson disagreed with those who hold that the work of ARCIC I was a mere papering over of the cracks. He stated that the method of ignoring development in the later Middle Ages, in the Reformation and the Counter-Reformation, and 'returning to a consideration of doctrine in the biblical and patristic periods' was right and 'fruitful to an extraordinary degree, and will in the end, in my opinion, create a climate of opinion in which reunion will be almost unavoidable'.[42] Seeing that this is always how Anglicans claim to have done theology, can we doubt the profitable relevance of the continuing Anglican identity to the ending of the pain and scandal of Christian disunity? There could not be a clearer contemporary endorsement of the threefold dialectic than Hanson's when he wrote 'We are not called to jettison Scripture as an historical check on this development (i.e. of doctrine); on the contrary, it is vital to retain it as a norm and not simply as a base . . . Scripture can and must be used as a norm, but used with flexibility and breadth of understanding, and we must not flinch from some of the more disturbing consequences which flow from these principles . . . Tradition must indeed remain as a criterion. We cannot start Christianity again from a *tabula rasa*, nor from the Bible alone, nor wholly and consistently from any past point in history . . . But we must be prepared to reexamine and reassess tradition'. He concludes that 'if we are to understand properly the continuity of Christian doctrine we are driven to seek for a properly flexible and comprehensive concept of the Church'.[43]

The affirmation of the continuing identity of Anglicanism is no crude assertion of denominationalism but the modest insistence that the Church which has brought us to *where we are* as Anglicans has a vocation of responsibility in company with other traditions to help to bring us all as fellow-Christians to *where we should be* in the unity for which Christ prayed. We have been listening to voices from our past and who can say that they are not evoking clear echoes and resonances in our present?

NOTES

1. The Anglican Ethos

1 H. R. McAdoo, *The Unity of Anglicanism: Catholic and Reformed* (Connecticut, 1983), p. 10.
2 loc. cit., pp. 14–15.
3 *Opuscula* (L.A.C.T.ed.), p. 91.
4 R. J. Page, *New Directions in Anglican Theology* (1965), p. 34.
5 H. R. McAdoo, *Being an Anglican* (London and Dublin, 1977), p. 6.
6 *A Relation of the Conference* (3rd. ed.), Preface.
7 Norman Sykes, *William Wake* (Cambridge, 1957), Vol.I, p. 163.
8 Jeremy Taylor *(Works,* ed. Heber), Vol. XI, p. 185.
9 *Report*, p. 64.
10 ib. p. 63.
11 R. P. C. Hanson, *Continuity of Christian Doctrine* (New York 1981), pp. 29, 77, 83: *Authority in the Anglican Communion* (Toronto 1987 ed. Stephen Sykes), H. R. McAdoo, pp. 78–82.
12 A. M. Ramsey, *The Gospel and the Catholic Church* (London, 1937), p. 64.
13 *Life of H. P. Liddon,* by J. O. Johnston, p. 134.
14 See also, H. R. McAdoo, *Being an Anglican* (1977), pp. 13–15.
15 Quoted in *Anglicanism* (1935), ed. More and Cross, p. 132.
16 *The Conference,* (1901 ed. by C. H. Simkinson), xiv, 385, and cf. 379.
17 William Payne (1650–1696), quoted in *Anglicanism,* p. 141.
18 The epistle dedicatory to *A Discourse of the Liberty of Prophesying* (1647).
19 See *Christian Authority* (ed. G. R. Evans, Oxford, 1988), H. R. McAdoo 'The influence of the Seventeenth Century', pp. 269–271. The reference to Laud is *Conference,* ii, 50, and to Wake, Sykes, loc. cit., I, pp. 254, 262–4, 297.
20 *Pattern of Catechistical Doctrine (1630),* Part I, C. ii, (2).
21 *Report,* p. 82.
22 E. P. II. VIII. 5.
23 E. P. V. VI–VIII.
24 E. P. II. VII, 6.
25 See W. Hamilton's *Life* of James Bonnell (1707).
26 G. Vann, *St. Thomas Aquinas* (1940), p. 91.
27 *Conference,* xiv, 385 and 379.
28 ib., iii, 86.
29 ib. x, 292.
30 See the close of the *Conference.*
31 E. C. E. Bourne, *The Anglicanism of William Laud* (London 1947), pp. 144–6.
32 *The Golden Remains of the Ever-memorable Mr John Hales* (3rd impression), p. 18.

33 Hales, loc. cit., p. 3.
34 ib. p. 31.
35 *Collection of Several Philosophical Writings (1662)*, Preface General, p. vi.
36 H. R. McAdoo, *The Spirit of Anglicanism* (London and New York, 1965), p. 81.
37 *Doctor Dubitantium*, Rule III (22), p. 434, Vol. XI (Heber ed.).
38 *A Discourse of the Liberty of Prophesying*, Sect. X, 5. (*Works*, ed. Heber, Vol. VIII, pp. 97–8)
39 *Works*, (Heber ed.), Vol. V, 498, Vol. XI, 485.
40 E. Fowler, *The Principles and Practices of certain Moderate Divines ... abusively called Latitudinarians* (22nd ed. 1671), Pt. I, p. 10.
41 Stillingfleet, *A Rational Account* (1681 ed.), ii, 41.
42 ib. Preface, pp, 188–9.
43 *Church Times*, 30/11/90.
44 The Lambeth Conferences (1867–1930) (London 1948), pp. 113–4.
45 *Religio Medici* (1643), Sect. 5. (1964 ed., pp. 5–6, ed. L. C. Martin).

2. The People in the Pews

1 Robert South, *Sermons* (1698), Vol. III, pp. 274–82.
2 For some facts and figures, see, for example, F. R. Bolton, *The Caroline Tradition of the Church of Ireland* (1958), pp. 182–197.
3 *Religio Medici*, I (xxx).
4 See *The Mathematical and Philosophical Works of the Rt. Rev. John Wilkins* (1802 ed.) Vol. I, p. 13, Vol. II, p. 188.
5 *Of the Principles and Duties of Natural Religion* (1675), First Book, C. III, p. 30.
6 *Religio Medici*, I (i).
7 C. H. Herford in his introduction to the *Everyman* edition (1945), p. xiii, of the *Religio Medici*. The most recent edition (Oxford, 1964) of *Religio Medici and Other Works* is by L. C. Martin.
8 R. M. II (11).
9 R. M. I (i).
10 R. M. I (45).
11 R. M. I (3). He rejects those who 'confine the Church' and have made it 'far narrower than our Saviour ever meant it'. ib. (55).
12 R. M. I (5).
13 R. M. I (6).
14 R. M. I (3).
15 R. M. I (9).
16 R. M. I (15).
17 R. M. I (36).
18 R. M. I (58).
19 R. M. I (60).
20 R. M. I (15).
21 R. M. II (7).
22 R. M. II (1).
23 R. M. II (8).

24 R. M. II (i).
25 R. M. II (13).
26 C. M. I (vi).
27 C. M. III (xxi).
28 C. M. I (iii).
29 C. M. I (xii).
30 C. M. III (xiv).
31 C. M. II (iii, v).
32 C. M. III (30).
33 R. M. II (12).
34 *The Diary of John Evelyn* for 17–18 October 1671.
35 *The Exemplary Life and Character of James Bonnell, Esq. Late Accomptant General of Ireland* (3rd ed. London, 1709, pp. 39, 54) by William Hamilton.
36 *Life*, pp. v–vii.
37 *Life*, pp. 254, 247.
38 *Life*, p. 242.
39 *Life*, p. 212.
40 *Life*, p. xiii.
41 *Life*, p. 209.
42 *Life*, p. 215.
43 *St. Bernard's Sermons on the Song of Songs* (1920 ed.), Vol. I, p. 144.
44 *Life*, p. 132.
45 *True Catholic and Apostolic Faith maintained in the Church of England* (New ed. 1840), p. 203.
46 F. R. Bolton, *The Caroline Tradition of the Church of Ireland* (1958), p. 194.
47 ib. p. 193 and for La Touche, see Judith Flannery, *The Story of Delgany* (Dublin, 1990), p. 43.
48 *Life*, p. 105.
49 *Life*, pp. 5-6.
50 *Life*, pp. 150–7.
51 *Life*, pp. 162–5.
52 *Life*, pp. 166–7, 176–7.
53 *The Windsor Statement* (8).
54 *Life*, pp. 94–6.
55 loc. cit., p. 196.
56 *Life*, pp. 112–120, 207.
57 *Life*, pp. 135, 244.
58 *Life*, pp. 222–5, 239.
59 *The Diary of Samuel Pepys* (1970, ed. Robert Latham and William Matthews), Vol. I, pp. cxix–cxx.

3. More People in the Pews

1 See her introduction to the Everyman edition (1964 reprint) of *The Compleat Angler*, p. xii.
2 *Thomas Ken: Bishop and Non-juror* (1958), by H. A. L. Rice, pp. 51–2.
3 loc. cit., p. xi.

4 *The Compleat Angler*, The Fourth Day.
5 *The Compleat Angler*, The Epistle to the Reader.
6 See The First Day and The Fourth Day.
7 Roger Pilkington, *Robert Boyle: Father of Chemistry* (London 1959)
8 loc. cit., p. 54.
9 For an assessment of Boyle's scientific achievements, see Pilkington, pp. 127–160; for an evaluation of his influence on theology, see my *The Spirit of Anglicanism* (1965) pp. 261–285.
10 quoted in Pilkington, p. 70.
11 *Occasional Reflections upon Several Subjects* (2nd ed. 1669); Introductory Preface and Letter.
12 loc. cit., Sect. III, C. VI.
13 *The Diary of John Evelyn*, entry for 11th April 1656.
14 ib. Entry for 6th January 1692.
15 *Diary*, 12th November 1642.
16 ib., 9th April – 5th May, 1645.
17 ib. 5th June 1650.
18 ib. October 4th, 1647.
19 ib. December, 1648.
20 ib. 30th January 1649.
21 ib. 5th June 1650 and cp. 28th July 1660: 'most of the Bishops in all 3 Kingdome, being now almost worn out, and *Sees* vacant'.
22 R. S. Bosher. *The Making of the Restoration Settlement* (London 1951), pp. 90 ff.
23 Bramhall, *Works* (L.A.C.T.ed.), I, p. 276.
24 ib. 29th August 1651.
25 ib. 1st Feb. 1652.
26 ib. 10th February 1652.
27 ib. 26th January 1655.
28 ib. 31st March 1655.
29 ib. 25th December 1656.
30 ib. 15th April 1655.
31 ib. 8th June 1688.
32 ib. 6th October 1688.
33 *Dictionary of National Biography*.
34 David Siegenthaler in *Anglican Spirituality* (1982), ed. William J. Wolf.
35 A. Tindal Hart, *The Man in the Pew* (London 1966), p. 192 and see Horton Davies *Worship and Theology in England* (Princeton Press and O.U.P.), Vol. I, pp. 440–1.
36 loc. cit. pp. 193–7.
37 Quotations from Taylor, *Works* (Heber ed.), Vol. 6, pp. 470–480.

4. Anglican Spirituality – the liturgical and moral-ascetical components

1 Martin Thornton, *English Spirituality* (London 1963), p. xiii.
2 *Anglican Spirituality* (Connecticut, 1982), p. iv.

3 *Anglican Spirituality*, p. 105.
4 ib. p. 18.
5 *What is Anglicanism?* (Connecticut, 1982), pp. 79–71.
6 *The Anglican Spiritual Tradition* (London, 1983), p. 110.
7 *The Diary of Samuel Pepys*, for 4th and 11th November 1660.
8 *The Diary of John Evelyn*, for 5th October 1656.
9 J. R. H. Moorman, loc. cit., p. 126.
10 *The Exemplary Life and Character of James Bonnell*, (1709 ed.), p. 191. Hamilton says the religious societies 'which gave Bonnell great comfort and joy' began in Dublin 'about the year 1693'.
11 *Anglican Spirituality*, p. vi.
12 *Eikon Basilike* C 16. John Gauden, bishop of Exreter, is thought by many to be the likely author but this is not certain.
13 *English Spirituality* (London 1963), pp. 76, 231.
14 *Anglican Spirituality* (Connecticut, 1982), pp. 6–7.
15 G. W. O. Addleshaw and Frederick Etchells, *The Architectural Setting of Anglican Worship* (London 1958), p. 22.
16 John Cosin, *Notes and Collections on the Book of Common Prayer* (1710, posthumously); Sparrow, *A Rationale or Practical Exposition of the Book of Common Prayer* (1657); L'Estrange *The Alliance of Divine Offices* (1659).
17 Preface, pp. xv–xvi.
18 ib. pp. vii–ix.
19 *Anglican Spirituality*, pp. 107, 111.
20 *English Spirituality*, p. 263.
21 *A Companion to the Temple*, II, pp. 60, 93.
22 *A Companion for the Festivals and Fasts of the Church of England*, Preface, p. ii.
23 loc. cit., p. 622.
24 loc. cit., Vol. I, p. 65.
25 *Holy Living*, Chap. II, 1.
26 For a good deal of what follows I draw upon my book *The Structure of Caroline Moral Theology* (London 1949), Ch. VI, 'The Spiritual Life in the English Church' and on my chapter in *The Anglican Moral Choice*, (ed. Paul Elmen, Connecticut 1983), 'Anglican Moral Theology in the Seventeenth Century: An Anticipation'.
27 Sermon III Ad Clerum, n. 34; Vol II, p. 105 and cp. Sermon IX Ad Aulam, n. 28, Vol. I, p. 242 (Oxford 1884).
28 *Unum Necessarium*, Preface and C. III, 1.
29 *Human Values and Christian Morality* (1970), p. 3.
30 *A New Introduction to Moral Theology* (1964), p. 28.
31 *Unum Necessarium*, Ch. II, Sect. II.
32 *The Law of Christ*, I, p. 72.
33 *Unum Necessarium*, Ch. II, Sect. I.
34 *A Practical Discourse of Repentance*, Chap. I, Sect. III.
35 *Sermons and Discourses* (1716), Sermon VII.
36 See the first of the Exhortations preparatory to Holy Communion in the *Book of Common Prayer*: 'If there be any of you, who . . . cannot quiet his

own conscience herein, but requireth further comfort or counsel, let him come to me, or to some other discreet and learned Minister of God's Word, and open his grief; that by the ministry of God's holy Word, he may receive the benefit of absolution, together with spiritual counsel and advice . . .'.

37 See *The Structure of Caroline Moral Theology* (1949), Chap. V.
38 *Works* (Oxford, 1829), Vol. V, Sermon XI.
39 *Unum Necessarium*, Ch. III, Sect. 4.
40 ib. Ch. III.
41 See *The Structure of Caroline Moral Theology* (1949) Chap. IV. for a full treatment of the subject.
42 *Golden Remains of the Ever Memorable Mr John Hales* (1659), the second sermon on the profit of godliness.

5. Anglican Spirituality – a distinctive character.

1 D. A. Chart in *History of the Church of Ireland* (ed. Walter Alison Phillips, 1933), Vol. III, p. 240.
2 *The Study of Anglicanism* (ed. Sykes and Booty, London 1988), p. 322.
3 *Masters of English Theology*, p. 105.
4 Paul A. Welsby, *Lancelot Andrewes* (London 1958), p. 266.
5 There is a modern edition (1967), ed. P. G. Stanwood.
6 *Christian Consolations*, Chap. IV.
7 ib. Chap. V.
8 ib. Chap. IV.
9 ib. Chap. V.
10 ib. Chap. IV.
11 Nelson, *The Practice of True Devotion* (1698), Chap. XV.
12 Hamilton's *Life*, p. 172 and see also pp. 168–170.
13 *The Great Exemplar* (Heber ed. Vol. II, p. ixv.)
14 loc. cit. Exhortation to the Imitation (15), ib. p. lxix.
15 *The Great Necessity and Advantage of Frequent Communion*, (posthumously in 1710), *Works*, L.A.C.T. ed. Vol. III, p. 604.
16 'Prayers before Receiving of the Blessed Sacrament'.
17 *The Great Exemplar*, Sect. V, Discourse III, of Meditation.
18 loc. cit., Chap. I.
19 ib. See Chaps. II, VI, VII, X, XI, XVI, XVII.
20 *Heaven upon Earth*, Sect. XXIV. See also *The Balm of Gilead*, Sects. IX–XV.
21 *The Devout Soul*, Sect. XXII.
22 *Practice of True Devotion*, Chap. XVI.
23 *The Christian Manuell* (1576), ed. The Parker Society, pp. 30–2, 101.
24 *The Practice of Piety* ed. Grace Webster (London 1842).
25 Twenty-two Sermons (1801 ed.) Vol. II, Sermon XXII, p. 532.
26 *The Whole Duty of Man*, Sunday III (12).
27 Quoted in J. R. H. Moorman, loc. cit., p. 128.
28 Quoted in *The Structure of Caroline Moral Theology*, p. 155.

29 R. S. Bosher, *The Making of the Restoration Settlement* (1951), pp. 36–7.
30 Sunday I (37).
31 Sunday I (23).
32 To the Christian Reader, The Private Devotion.
33 *The Great Exemplar*, Pt. I, sect. III and Pt. III, sect. XV.
34 *Holy Living*, Chap. IV, Sect. III.
35 *Holy Living*, Chap. IV, Sect. IX.
36 *Holy Living*, Chap. IV, Sect. X.
37 See Chap. XIII and Preface.
38 *Ecclesiastical Polity*, V, 18.
39 See *A Priest to the Temple, or, The Country Parson* (1652), Chap. XXI.
40 *Diary*, 2nd November, 1656.
41 Epistle dedicatory in his *Plain and Full Exposition*.
42 To the Reader, p. v.
43 Beveridge, *The Church Catechism Explained* (1704) Preface.
44 *Plain and Full Exposition of the Catechism* (1655), section on the decalogue.
45 Henry Hammond's *Practical Catechism*, Lib. I, Sect. III.

6. Postscript from the Present

 1 Robert Hale, *Canterbury and Rome, Sister Churches* (London 1982), p. 16.
 2 Preface, *Baptism, Eucharist and Ministry* (1982)
 3 *The Conversation at Malines* (Oxford, 1927), p. 44.
 4 ib., pp. 38, 40.
 5 e.g. *Final Report* (1982), pp. 5, 12, 17; *Lima Report* (1982), p. 8.
 6 'Anglican/Roman Catholic Dialogue' in *One in Christ* (Vol. VIII, No. 3, 1972)
 7 *The Conversations at Malines* (1930), p. 22.
 8 *Fisher of Lambeth* (London 1969), by William Purcell, p. 283.
 9 W. H. Van de Pol, *Anglicanism in Ecumenical Perspective* (1965), p. 34.
10 Michael Marshall, *The Anglican Church Today and Tomorrow* (1984), p. 140.
11 *From Gore to Temple* (1960), p. ix.
12 *Some Considerations Touching the Style of the Holy Scriptures* (1661), *Works* (1772), Vol. II, p. 260.
13 All quotations from Laud's *A Relation of the Conference* (1639). He insists on the principle that 'tradition doth but morally and probably confirm the authority of Scripture'.
14 *Origines Sacrae*, Preface to the Reader, 7th ed. 1702.
15 *A Rational Account* (1687 ed.), Chap. II, p. 41.
16 ib., p. 596.
17 ib., p. 189.
18 ib. Chap. IV, p. 91.
19 ib. p. 243.
20 *Sermons on the Incarnation* (1693), Vol. I, Sermon II, p. 63.
21 See Vol. IV, V.
22 ib. Vol. I, p. 68.

23 quoted in *Anglicanism* (1935, ed. More & Cross), p. 116.
24 *Ductor Dubitantium*, Rule III (64), *Works* (Heber ed.), Vol. XI, pp. 462–3.
25 *Select Discourses* (2nd ed. 1673); see Discourses I, IV, VII, VIII. Smith died in 1652, aged thirty-four, and the *Discourses* were published posthumously.
26 *Unum Necessarium*, Ch. VI, Section IV (16) and Ch. VI, Section I (36), *Works* (Heber ed.), Vol. IX, pp. 17, 40.
27 *Ductor Dubitantium*, Rule III (23)–(24), *Works* (Heber ed.), Vol. XI, p. 442.
28 Section IV (1).
29 ib. Section IV (8).
30 ib. Section VI (1).
31 ib. Section VI (12).
32 ib. Section V (8) and (11).
33 *Works*, (Heber ed. Vol. VII, pp. xvii–xix).
34 *Golden Remains of the Ever Memorable Mr John Hales* (3rd impression, 1687), pp. 27, 31.
35 J. Morley, *The Life of W. E. Gladstone* (1903), III, p. 480.
36 *Discourse of the Liberty of Prophesying*, Section X, (5).
37 *Theology*, Vol. XCIII March/April 1990, No. 752, pp. 99–101.
38 As reported in the *Church Times* for 28 March 1991.
39 loc. cit., pp. 155–6.
40 John Bramhall, *Works* (in a collected edition, 1676), pp. 61, 101, 141, 439, 407, 625.
41 Full text of the study-document in the *Information Service* of the PCPCU, N. 74, 1990 (111).
42 loc. cit., pp. 68–9.
43 ib. pp. 82–3, 88.